DON'T GO IN THAT ROOM!

A Girlfriend's Guide
to Avoiding Dating and Relationship
Hell

ANNETTE MARIE WESTWOOD
The Beverly Hills Eulogy

Copyright © 2016, Annette Marie Westwood
All rights reserved. No part of this publication may be reproduced, distributed, or transmitted in any form or by any means, including photocopying, recording, or other electronic or mechanical methods, without the prior written permission of the publisher, except in the case of brief quotations embodied in critical reviews and certain other noncommercial uses permitted by copyright law. For permission requests, write to the publisher at the address below:

Annette Marie Westwood

Editing by Cara Highsmith, Highsmith Creative Services, www.highsmithcreative.com

Some names and identifying details have been changed to protect the privacy of individuals.

Although the author and publisher have made every effort to ensure that the information in this book was correct at press time, the author and publisher do not assume and hereby disclaim any liability to any party for any loss, damage, or disruption caused by errors or omissions, whether such errors or omissions result from negligence, accident, or any other cause.

This book is not intended as a substitute for the medical advice of physicians. The reader should regularly consult a physician in matters relating to his/her health and particularly with respect to any symptoms that may require diagnosis or medical attention.

The information in this book is meant to supplement, not replace, proper (name your sport) training. Like any sport involving speed, equipment, balance and environmental factors, (this sport) poses some inherent risk. The authors and publisher advise readers to take full responsibility for their safety and know their limits. Before practicing the skills described in this book, be sure that your equipment is well maintained, and do not take risks beyond your level of experience, aptitude, training, and comfort level.

ISBN-13 - 978-0-9984584-0-3
ISBN-13 (eBook) - 978-0-9984584-1-0
Printed in the United States of America
First Edition 16 15 14 13 12 11 10 / 10 9 8 7 6 5 4 3 2 1

CONTENTS

INTRODUCTION
Be Afraid; Be Very Afraid

PART I: IMAGINE YOUR WORST FEAR A REALITY
Signs You're Heading into Danger

CHAPTER ONE: Don't Go in that Room!
What You Should Be Watching Out For

CHAPTER TWO: If You Think You're Safe, You're Dead Wrong
Dating Under the Influence

CHAPTER THREE: You Have Been Warned
Separating the Boys from the Men

PART II: JUST WHEN YOU THOUGHT IT WAS SAFE TO GO BACK INTO THE WATER
Finding Your Way Out of the Woods

CHAPTER FOUR: It's Only a Movie ... It's Only a Movie
You Are in Control

CHAPTER FIVE: When the Lights Go Out the Terror Begins
The Smart Rules for Sex and Dating

CHAPTER SIX: I Warned You Not to Go Out Tonight
What's Done is Done, But You Can Learn from It

CHAPTER SEVEN: Think You're Alone? Think Again
You Can't Force it if He Doesn't Like You, Pretty Flower

PART III: THEY'RE BAACKK!!
How to Avoid Getting Dragged Back In

CHAPTER EIGHT: The Next Scream You Hear May Be Your Own
Masturbation and Other Self-Preservation Tactics

CHAPTER NINE: Checking In Is Easy; Checking Out is Hell
Being Prepared for a Break-up

CHAPTER TEN: Who Will Survive and What Will Be Left of Them?
Getting Closure and Moving On

ACKNOWLEDGMENTS

This book is dedicated to
all the beautiful flowers looking for love
and all the good men who know what love is.

INTRODUCTION

"Be Afraid; Be Very Afraid"
—*The Fly*

What the hell happened to dating? When did the thrill of dating turn into one of those terrifying thrillers where no one makes it out without some level of trauma? You know what I mean. Think of how many times you've come home from a date calling it a nightmare. I bet every woman you know has a horror story of a boyfriend or a husband who made their lives a living hell.

When did a lot of women stop allowing men to open doors, pull out chairs, and generally offer them help? And why? Don't we all love romance and chivalry? Why are we considered bad feminists if we allow a man to be nice to us? The dating and relationship world has changed, and not for the better. So, who is to blame? I bet you'd like to put it all on the guys who've just turned into soul-sucking monsters, but I'm sorry to say we bear some of the responsibility, pretty Flowers. Some women lost their self-confidence and have resorted to chasing men, asking them out, paying for dinner and drinks, going out of their way to meet for a date.

Some accept the bone he throws for a last-minute date request when he doesn't have anything better to do. Some women date married men like it's okay. Some look the other way when men cheat on them. Some women sleep with men on the first date, essentially risking their heart and health for a stranger that didn't prove himself worthy. Women who want to get married, move in with men without the commitment, essentially auditioning to become their wives. And what has this behavior done? It's made dating a full on nightmare for all the good ladies out there looking for love and commitment.

The online dating game has some positives, but also caused an epidemic of bad behavior. Men got the memo that they don't have to do anything to have the sex, and it has spread like the Bubonic Plague. It's made the bad men worse and the good men give up on finding a good woman. Too many of us are not acting like good women or have stopped acting like good women because men aren't acting like real men.

A man can go online and find a different woman to take out for dinner or drinks and have the sex with every night. A confident and persuasive man can even convince a woman to cover the bill and still give up the sex without his having to do anything.

The problem is, when women got sick of men cheating on and lying to them, they started to play the game too. Unfortunately, all that accomplished was conditioning our victims to treat the next woman poorly because they felt used and their needs weren't met. It's a crazy cycle.

It's kind of like what we see in a horror film. We know damn well that danger lurks inside that rundown shack in the woods. We can see the crazy train coming when one of the characters says, "I'm going to go check out that dark basement." Hollywood has even made spoofs out of how predictably the characters make bad choices that lead to tragic outcomes. But, we don't have to keep making the same stupid choices in our romantic lives.

Don't Go in that Room! is a humorous relationship guide for women who want a good man who thinks they are like butter. Being treated like butter means you are respected, cherished, and savored. Women, you should be treated this way and never settle for less. And, at the risk of throwing another metaphor at you, you deserve to be treated like the beautiful Flower that you are. Yes, I call women Flowers because they are delicate and unique, but resilient and can weather a lot of storms.

This is a guide for women who are fabulous but are continuing to make mistakes that get them hurt in relationships—women who can't seem to find that good man or haven't found the humor in this crazy game of love. The key to dating survival is finding the humor in it.

Don't Go in that Room! will help you to tell the difference between a good man and a shitty man; but, even more important, you'll learn how to stop yourself from going there with the bad ones in spite of all the signs.

With this guide I'm going to take you through the dark and scary places into the light of day where everything will be clearer and more hopeful. We're going to start by looking at all the clues that tell you you're heading into danger—the dark woods, scary cemeteries, and haunted houses you pass on your way home. We'll talk about why, just as the characters in horror films, we look at a scenario we know we shouldn't explore, but run in head-first anyway.

Then we will get into the thick of it where we deal with the nightmares you may already be in and can't find your way out of. I'll help you understand what you're doing to make things worse and which doors actually lead you to safety. Once we're there, we will do what is necessary to destroy those evil spirits that threaten to drag you back in.

In scary movies, there's always that goblin or zombie that raises its head up one last time to let you know the danger still lurks. But, if you apply what you've learned, you'll have nothing to fear.

And, men, even though I am speaking primarily to women in this book, I think there is useful information for you here as well. Maybe you are a gay man running into the same types of problems dating men that women do. Maybe you are a straight man wanting to better understand what women need out of relationships. Either way, I hope you will take te time to read this with an open mind and see what you can do to help take the fear out of this madness called dating.

There is no reason our love lives have to be frightening experiences. Come into the light with me ... and I don't mean the one calling to Carol Ann! (That was a Poltergeist reference for those of you who aren't horror fans.) You really can have a great dating life that leads to a happy marriage, but you have to stop making stupid and totally avoidable mistakes. Let me show you how, pretty Flower!

—Annette Marie

PART I

"Imagine Your Worst Fear a Reality"
—*The Howling*

Signs You're Heading Into Danger

CHAPTER ONE
"Don't Go in that Room!"

What You Should Be Watching Out For

So, you're sitting in your recliner, eating your movie theatre butter popcorn with a lot of salt. You're curled up in your comfy chair and the dumb girl in the movie is about to go into the house. You can't even stand it as she pushes open the creaky door and looks around. You have to cover your eyes when she looks down the long dark hallway to another door with a light shining under it, and all you can think is, *Stop! How do you not know the killer is waiting for you? You are so going to die!*

You wonder why her intuition wasn't telling her not to go into the house. Surely she could feel something was wrong. I mean, she was moving slowly, being cautious, looking around. She sees things aren't okay—the out of service landline, the dead cell phone, the cobwebs and broken floor boards—but she still keeps walking toward that door. You jump up, spilling your over-salted popcorn and yell, "ARE YOU CRAZY? DON'T GO IN THAT ROOM!"

Sound familiar? We've all been there. But, beyond the horror films, I've been there when I see women breaking common-sense dating rules. When I hear about a woman compromising her standards to get a date, I want to shout, "Don't go in that room!" If she is driving halfway to meet them, paying for dates, giving her lady center away too quickly, dating under the influence, or making excuses for their behavior, she is voluntarily walking into a nightmare scenario.

I know the statistics on how it's going to end, and it's rarely good. Getting hurt in this game of love is par for the course, but that's why I want to help you set yourself up to win the game, not lose. I don't want to see you open those doors that lead to danger or wander down those dark, scary trails where creeps lurk.

You've probably seen a list of the top things characters do wrong in horror films. I'm going to give you some simple rules for dating based on the worst mistakes made in scary movies so you can have an easier time venturing out there, finding the man of your dreams, and avoiding relationship nightmares.

RULE 1 – NEVER CHASE AFTER YOUR PET

You've seen it so many times. Fluffy or Spot scratches at the door and is acting weird. Our girl opens the door to let them out and they run off into the darkness. She runs after her pet (barely dressed in a skimpy nightie, of course) to bring them back into the yard. I don't have to tell you what happens next, right?

Well, let me make this clear from the beginning, ladies: Don't chase after men! Don't ask them out. Let men ask you out. Some of my friends completely disagree with me on this and do ask men on dates. Sometimes it works and they say yes. They might even get a boyfriend out of it. But, they also learn in time that I'm still right! They end up finding out that they set a bad precedent by making the first move.

Chapter One

These women let their guy think he didn't have to do any of the work in the relationship and they eventually woke up to the realization that they were dating a boy, not a man. The truth is, if a man doesn't have the balls to ask you out, he isn't going to have what it takes to do the heavy lifting when your relationship gets hard.

But, this doesn't mean you sit back and wait for someone to drop in your lap either. There are things you can, and should, do. It is okay to drop the handkerchief, so to speak. Flirting is important for setting the stage. You have to be open and receptive so they get the hint. But, you have to let them ask—let them chase you. They will if they like you.

Here are a few tips to communicate your availability without seeming desperate or too available:

- If you're on an online dating site, click "wink" or "like" on his photo. If he is interested, he will get in touch with you.
- If you're at the grocery store or a bar, make conversation, let him see how great you are, and he will ask you out if he can't get enough.
- If you're at a party together, ask a mutual friend to introduce you, and then dazzle him with your winning personality. If he wants to see you again, he won't let you get away without asking for your number.

If you have to beg for the attention of a man, it isn't worth the little bit he gives you. You deserve to have a man who will move heaven and earth to convince you to give him a shot; not a pussy who can't ask you out!

RULE 2 - NEVER GO WHERE YOU'LL BE TRAPPED

How many times have you watched our girl in a scary movie run into the basement or into an alley where she is bound to be trapped? She hits a dead end and looks around trying to figure out how the hell she got in that situation. Well, I'm here to tell you, the same thing can happen in dating if you aren't careful.

Obviously, your safety is the priority, so make good choices for that reason alone; but, in addition to that, you have to be aware of what you are doing when you decide where to have a first date. Once you have his attention and a date with him, don't screw it up by compromising on how you should be treated. He asked you to spend time with him, so he should come to you and be willing to go wherever is best and most convenient for you.

That means no meeting him on his turf, no driving to his area of town, no going out of your way. If this is a first date, keep yourself safe and consider meeting him somewhere close to your office or your neighborhood. You are laying the groundwork for the future of a potential relationship. Don't skimp on the things you want to get out of it.

Remember you teach men how to treat you. If you meet him halfway at the beginning, you will spend the rest of your relationship giving in to his needs and only getting half of what you need. (NOTE: This is different from the kind of compromises you reach in relationships down the road, such as where you live, how many kids you have, who stays home with them, etc.)

If he isn't willing to put in the effort to see you at the beginning, what kind of relationship do you think you'll have later on? If he isn't willing to go out of his way during the phase when he's under the most pressure to make a good impression, what do you expect to get when he's confident you aren't going anywhere? You're worth the drive for a man. If you don't think that's true, stop dating and work on some self-love.

RULE 3 – NEVER GET CAUGHT UNPREPARED

Every horror film has one common mistake that every character commits: not being prepared. Whether it's failing to keep the car in good shape, not having batteries for the flashlight, or having bad cellphone service, not having the basics for being able to call for help or help herself is the quickest way for our girl to end up dead.

If you have made it this far, you've been asked out and made arrangements for him to come to you. That's great! You've made it past two major traps. But don't get lost on the way to safety by making a bad choice on planning the date. Dating is not nearly as dangerous as getting stranded in the haunted woods, but not having some good suggestions ready can be the death of your date, and possibly the future of a new relationship.

Whether you met a man online or In Real Life (IRL), if he asks you for date suggestions, give him three choices of things you like to do in your area that are free or really inexpensive. Remember, this is a meet and greet. Don't get yourself committed to more than you can get out of gracefully should you need to escape. If things go well, you can always keep going.

The important thing is to: 1) select a place that is convenient to you, 2) find something interesting to do where you aren't entirely dependent on being an expert conversationalist, and 3) keep it open-ended, but start with a time limit.

HELPFUL HINT: Museums are great dating place. You can walk around and look at art while you're getting to know each other. Outdoor shopping centers are another great place. You don't have to sit and stare at each other and think of things to talk about, or feel like you're being interviewed.

RULE 4 - NEVER READ FROM THE SCARY BOOK

We all know how demon possession turns the mild-mannered neighbor into a raving lunatic. It usually happens when one of the morons in the group picks up some creepy old book and starts reading the strange language on the page. Soon one of their friends is not acting like themselves, and before you know it they are destroying everything.

Well, there is big danger for you to get into some crazy behavior of your own if you break my rule of not drinking on a first date. We'll get into this more later, but I don't think I can say this enough: be fully present and aware on your meet and greet. Would you ever go to job interview and drink? No, you would not (unless you're an alcoholic). The biggest decision you will ever make is choosing a husband, so it is essential that you make the decision sober. I know you're probably thinking, *It's just a first date! Who said anything about marriage?* But the reality is that every first date has the potential to become a relationship and that is when you will make the decision about whether this goes any further or stops there.

Sometimes people don't seem all that bad after a drink—especially if you haven't had sex in a while—and you might agree to a next date or a continuation of the current one when you shouldn't if your judgment is diminished by drinking. Your intuition can tell you a lot if you listen to it, but it doesn't work when it's impaired with alcohol. Get to know who he is without your beer goggles on.

RULE 5 - NEVER INVESTIGATE THE NOISE

There are certain instinctual, almost biological, things we see happen in male/female relationships, things we kind of expect. No, I'm not talking about sex. One example we see in horror movies is how we just know the guy in the group is going to volunteer to go check out that scary noise coming from the basement or the closet or the dark trail. He wants to protect and provide for everyone.

Men feel the need to hunt and kill things, and then bring them to you to take care of you in real life too. Let them. That means let the man pay for the date. In fact, insist on it. If a man's not willing to take care of you and make you feel special now, I cringe at the thought of your future with him.

Besides, as long as women are still earning seventy-eight cents for every dollar a man makes, the men can afford to buy the damn coffee with the twenty-two cent difference we are screwed out of.

Actually, I believe in doing things that are free for the first date, that way you won't feel so bad if it turns out you don't like him, and he isn't out any money if it doesn't go well.

Now, if you're an alpha-type female and want to take care of someone, there is nothing wrong with being the provider as long as he balances things by taking care of other aspects of your home and relationship. Just make sure you aren't supporting a freeloader or that you are with a man who won't feel emasculated by the role reversal.

The point is, let him be what his instinct leads him to want, then sit back and enjoy being pampered and treated like you are special.

RULE 6 – NEVER BE THE JERK

In scary movies, you can pretty much count on the fact that if a character is obnoxious, rude, insensitive, self-absorbed, or just generally an ass, he stands a good chance of coming to an especially gory end. While there's that part of you that feels bad because he is a human being, there is another small piece of you that is kind of glad he paid for being a jerk. So, the lesson here is don't be a jerk when you go on a date.

If you are asked out for dinner, please don't order

anything expensive. Be considerate. It's very inappropriate to allow a man spend money on you, especially if you don't think the relationship has potential.

I've heard too many men complain that the women they've dated would order a pricey three-course meal and then kick down two or three glasses of wine. That is just tacky. Feel free to do that with your husband or fiancé, but in dating that is bad form.

Let's be really blunt about the transaction that's actually happening in dating, shall we? He is buying you dinner as a down payment on companionship and sex, and if you're not going to give him those things in time, you shouldn't be accepting what he offers. It's kind of a crass, but widely understood, social contract, so it's really inappropriate to pretend you are agreeing to that if you don't intend for it to go in that direction.

I recognize that most men are not taking me out to dinner to make sure I've eaten because they are good people. They are not dating me because I write relationship books or throw Eulogies for people in transitions. They are on a date with me, first, because of my looks; second, because they want sex; third, because they don't want to eat alone; fourth, because they may want a relationship; and, fifth, probably because I pole dance. I'm not stupid.

But, you're with him to fulfill a need as well. Ask yourself: *What is my need?* I go out on dates to find the love of my life—the person that I want to spend my life with. The best way to make that a reality is to be very respectful and a high-value woman at all times. Don't ever use a man for dinner or drinks. It's no different from a man using you for sex. As women, let's not sink to that level. If you can't afford to pay for your own dinner you shouldn't be dating. You should be working on your career.

Chapter One

RULE 7 – DON'T GO SNOOPING

We see it in every horror film—our girl inevitably starts poking around out of curiosity and ends up releasing some evil creature or alerting the crazed killer to her hiding place. All of that could have been avoided if she had just stayed where it was safe and waited until the coast was clear.

How many times have you wandered into dangerous conversation territory on a date and really blown a good thing or made a bad situation worse? There are some topics that seem safe enough and end up hiding land mines you couldn't have expected, but there are some areas that just always hold potential disaster and it's best to steer clear of them.

Here are the big ones:
- *Exes* – If you tell him your ex is successful, he will feel intimated. Tell him your ex is a looser and he will think you date and marry losers. You can't win here. So, if a guy asks about your ex, say, "Why would I ever want to talk about him when I could get to know you?" See what we did there?
- *Therapists* – This screams baggage as loud as Jamie Lee Curtis in "Halloween," so, even if he tells you he has one, stay away from this topic. He will think you are Cray-Cray.
- *Politics* – Go ahead bring up Donald Trump; you will most likely get deported home. This is one of the most divisive topics of conversation you will find, and it's best to save this for a few dates down the road, if at all.
- *Religion* – This is the other most divisive topic you can bring up and talking about Jesus on a date will leave you at home still praying for a boyfriend. While religious background and beliefs may be important deciding factors for you, it's best to leave this for later,

once you've had a chance to get to know who they are.
- *Finances* – There was a time when you just didn't talk about money in polite company. Guys can be intimidated by independent women, so if you tell him you have money, he may think you're high-maintenance. Tell him you're poor and he may think you're a gold-digger. It's another no-win conversation topic.
- *Health Issues* – We all have some kind of ache, pain, or illness, but if you tell him you have IBS on a date he will think of you on the toilet instead of in the bedroom. In most cases, it's really not that interesting and can be another thing that sends up the red flag of baggage and drama.
- *Diet* – This could just be an LA thing, but everybody brings up their diet—*I'm Paleo, I'm Vegan, I'm Pegan.* I find it annoying. I eat cheeseburgers, candy, live on coffee, and drink diet soda. If I die from an overload of aspartame, I'm okay with that. I had a guy ask me if I liked my greens blended on a date. I told him I only like my margaritas blended. Turning your food order into a scene from *When Harry Met Sally* is only adorable in the movies. Being high-maintenance about your restaurant needs is a good way to guarantee you only get one date.

You may be thinking, *What the hell is there left to talk about?* Here, I'll give you some topics. Now, talk amongst yourselves …

FIVE-MINUTE CONVERSATIONS
- *Your Kids* - Men don't really want to know about their first words, trips to the dentist, dance classes, or medical issues. If you have little Johnny's primary tooth in your purse because it just fell out, don't show him! But, it is totally appropriate to share that you have

kids, their ages, and a little something about them; just keep his focus on you, not your kids.
- *Your Pets* – Please don't be that person who pulls out pictures or videos and talk about your dog or cat as though they are a child. If you show him your cat's Facebook page or your dog's two-hour YouTube video he may think you're Cray-Cray! That said, most people do like animals, so there is nothing wrong with finding out if they have any pets of their own, and then move on.
- *Your Friends* – Telling stories about people they don't know can get kind of weird because they can't relate. Look around you, especially if you live in NYC or LA; there are plenty of weirdos you can talk about. I had a 30-minute date conversation full of laughs about a forty-year-old man we saw on the street wearing Teenage Mutant Ninja Turtles pajamas, eating out of a box of Lucky Charms.
- *Your Job* – This topic has the potential to be a big yawn for the other person or a source of great conversation. Maybe if you're a crime scene cleaner you can elaborate a bit more. But, while it is an amazing and noble profession, if you're a nurse, there is no need to go on and on about taking blood pressure readings and giving shots—maybe one quick, funny story about the man who came in with a drill bit stuck in his hand. Just keep it short.

Dates where conversation just seems to flow easily without much effort are really exciting and pretty much guarantee a second date. The ones where you struggle to come up with something to talk about can feel like torture and not only will there not be another, you can't wait to escape the one you're on.

Unfortunately, sometimes a conversation misstep can tank a date that had the potential to be really great and you might miss the opportunity to connect with someone who is made for you. Don't let that happen. Keeping the conversation in the present, focusing on the things and people around you is the way to go. A woman should always keep the conversation light and fun and she should be a bit mysterious.

RULE 8 – NEVER SEEK HELP FROM THE CREEPY OLD GUY

You know the creepy old guy they have in nearly every scary movie who gives everyone an uneasy feeling they can't quite put their finger on? He doesn't do anything bad, but seems to know a little too much about the situation and is a little too helpful. He might turn out to be just kind of strange, but he might turn out to be the killer, and if that happens, the last thought our girl will have is, *Why didn't I listen to my gut?*

If you are on a date and you have a strong sense that this person is not right for you, put an end to the evening quickly. There is no point in dragging out something that just isn't going to work. Trust your gut!

Don't ever feel obligated to stick it out and stay on a date that doesn't feel right. I know you don't want to hurt a man's feelings, but it's honestly kind of selfish if you stay because you didn't just waste your time, you wasted theirs too. Let him go and find someone else. We all are busy people and really don't have time to humor someone we're not interest in, so don't do it.

Just be gracious about it. Say something like this: "I'm so sorry I overbooked myself today, I only have thirty minutes. I didn't want to be rude and cancel last minute." It's an honor to have a man want to go on a date with you whether he is right for you or not, so be kind, respectful, and lovely at all times.

Chapter One

RULE 9 – NEVER GO NEAR THE CLOWNS

Do you think clowns are creepy? Do you know anyone who doesn't? For something that is supposed to be fun and childlike, they are in a lot of horror films as the thing to be afraid of. It's pretty safe to say that whether they are scary or silly, clowns don't hold a lot of appeal for most people.

Clowning around in the dating scene is no better. That's a roundabout way of saying don't ever play games and don't tolerate them from the guy you're interested in either. It's so childish and doesn't help anyone.

If he is playing games with texts or phone calls, he's just not that interested, or else he's 50 going on 12. You know when a man likes you because he will jump in to save you from a serial killer or get rid of a poltergeist for you; no games will be necessary. Seriously, if you have to ask the question, "Does he like me?," the answer will always be no. You know the truth; you're not stupid.

And don't lead him on. Don't toy with him to keep him around to boost your ego or to have as a backup. Be direct and honest and let him know how you feel for better or worse. It saves a lot of time in the long run. It also helps to establish good communication in case this does turn into an actual relationship.

These are the rules most commonly broken early on in dating that have a huge impact on how a relationship develops or if it will at all. Just like the dumb moves people make in horror films, everyone on the outside looking in can totally see the disaster coming. They might be shouting warnings at you from afar or even be in your life telling you what you don't want to hear. Try to pick up on the signs that things might be heading in the wrong direction so you can avoid living out a nightmare.

Let's keep going and dig in to some of these a little further.

CHAPTER TWO

"If You Think You're Safe You're Dead Wrong"
—*The Prowler*

Dating Under the Influence

There are a few types of characters in horror films who will, no doubt, be the first to die, including the Drunk Girl, the "Know-it-All," and the Slow Runner. These are the stereotypically easy targets who end up sacrificed so the people who make it to the end can learn the dangers they are facing.

This chapter is about helping you figure out which of these you are so you can avoid being taken out of the game early. Drinking and dating sets you up for some really bad decisions. If you think you have it all figured out, you are going to end up being overconfident and make stupid mistakes. As the scapegoat, you are the fall guy, too weighed down by things you bring into the mix to get what you want out of dating.

We all have times when we might be one or another of these easy targets. Let's see if we can figure out whether you might be dating under the influence of some issue that will keep you from success. Are you the "Know-it-All" under the influence of ego, the Drunk Girl under the influence of alcohol, or the slow runner under the influence of other people's needs? Are you ready? It's time to get really honest with yourself.

The Drunk Girl

I don't understand why women would ever drink and date. I think it's just as bad as drinking and driving. Why would you go out with impaired judgment doing something that could potentially destroy your life. Making poor choices in dating may not seem life-altering, but think about it: the wrong decision on a date could lead to pregnancy, an STD, unsafe situations, not to mention the emotional fallout that comes from getting involved with the wrong guy.

Then there's the risk of DUI that involves enormous costs in attorneys, court fees, as well as damage to your record and reputation, and that's hoping you avoided hurting anyone in the process..

And let's not forget the nightmare of divorce. Many of the same costs are involved, but there is never a scenario where no one gets hurt.

I know it's not that simple, but any time alcohol is in the middle of the decision-making process, it rarely turns out well. Maybe you are stuck in a bad relationship that you don't know how to end and would never have chosen if you'd not been drinking on those first few dates.

Look, I understand that a nice glass of wine can take the edge off when you are out looking for love, but isn't it important to establish a real connection with a man? Don't you want to be able to have an intellectual conversation and get to know him, and see who he is? You can't do that very well if you are impaired, and even one drink can affect how your mind functions.

I know a lot of women who are really amazing, smart

women, but give them one cocktail and the inhibitions disappear like that first person down the stairs to investigate the scary noise. Unless you are out with a guy just looking for sex, being drunk is actually a turn-off to men. He certainly won't be considering you relationship material if you show him you can't control yourself around alcohol.

It's not a horror movie, per se, but have you ever seen *Blind Date* with Kim Basinger and Bruce Willis? She drinks on their first date and it turns into a total nightmare. Of course, Hollywood makes it turn out perfectly in the end. You aren't likely to be so lucky, so be smart and just leave the booze out of it when you are first dating so you can feel more confident in your decision. There will be plenty of time to celebrate after you have landed a wonderful, trustworthy, and stable guy!

The "Know-It-All"

Alcohol isn't the only influence that can impair your judgment. Sometimes we rush into things thinking we have it all figured out or we don't know what we want but can figure it out along the way. Don't let your over-confidence in your dating prowess get you into trouble.

Being a star doesn't always guarantee survival in scary movies. In fact, the super brainy people, the star football players, and the most popular cheerleaders are often the first to go. The last man or woman standing is usually the one who is able to use common sense to deal with whatever is thrown at them.

Being really attractive, having a great job, getting a great education, banking lots of money, and collecting lots of friends or followers mean nothing if you pick the wrong husband. Making a mistake in this most important decision of your life will end as badly as deciding to wander off into the dark, spooky woods alone. Especially if you end up having kids together because then you have to deal with this man for the rest of your life; it can be a life sentence of misery.

You worked hard getting your degree or climbing up the company ladder as a woman, so why would you get married to someone before you've done the research, spent enough time making sure he is the best fit for you and searching yourself to make sure you are ready?

Cindy
Cindy had a PhD and was gorgeous and smart—the full package, blessed with brains and beauty. But was she really blessed?

She had married a man who was not what he seemed. She thought he was a good man and it was time to settle down, so she ended up settling. Long story short and two kids later, she discovered that he wasn't a good fit for her and he wasn't a good man. She ended up divorced and alone. He has moved on to another wife, and her kids chose their father's side in the ugly battle. As smart and beautiful as she is, this woman is having a hard time with dating because she now comes with baggage.

It is so easy to fall into the trap of thinking because you look great on paper that you should have an easy time with finding love. But, being able to check all the boxes on the desired traits does not guarantee a good fit or success in dating. And you certainly can't settle because you feel it's time to get married.

Check your ego and your expectations at the door and try focusing on who you really are instead of all of your accomplishments or superficial qualities.

The Slow Runner

So, the slow runner is kind of a metaphor for anyone who is entering the dating race with some limitations. That might mean you have emotional baggage from a previous relationship, you are a single parent with limited time, or you just don't know what you want.

It's a scary time to wade into the dating waters, period; but, when you are under the influence of insecurities, distractions, and worries, it's a lot harder to keep up with all the competition. Let's see what we can do to get you up to speed.

BACK ON THE MARKET

If you're newly single you may not know about the horror of online dating yet. Well, buckle up your seatbelt; you're in for a real treat! Maybe your single friends have told you about the pain and agony of trying to find a healthy, stable, compatible person without fetishes or addictions, but it's another thing to experience it for yourself.

Online dating really is like shopping at stores like TJ Maxx or Marshall's—you have to go through tons of dresses to find the one beautiful designer dress you like that is also in your size. With online dating, you have to go through tons of profiles to find the one guy you may want to go out with, who may or may not be the right fit, and who may or may not be interested in you.

I want to help you manage your expectations going into online dating. I don't know anyone who has said they enjoyed online dating. They might have enjoyed meeting their husband or wife if they met online, but not the dating process itself.

In my opinion, before anyone gets divorced or wants to leave a long-term relationship, they should have to explore the online dating world for three months first. My guess is at least 75% would decide to work harder at the relationship they have.

Sadly, people make a big mistake thinking dating will be fun. It may, in fact, be worse than your last relationship; so don't set yourself up for failure. Don't have any expectations, that way, no matter how things go, you will end up happy.

But, you don't need to online date if you're not comfortable. There are other options! My advice is to put a little more effort into your appearance no matter where you go so you are always presenting an attractive first impression, then accept all invitations to go out, even when you don't feel like it. I guarantee you will meet men.

I highly recommend looking fabulous at the grocery store. Single men are always at the grocery store because they don't have a wife or girlfriend to get their stuff for them. And don't forget the park or the gym. You will definitely run into single guys there, so you want to look your best. I know achieving that level of perfection all the time is work, but guys are visual. If you go out looking like shit nobody is going to want to shag ya.

Although, you actually don't even need to go out of your house to get asked out. I've been approached by the locksmith who opened my door when I got locked out. The pest control man when it looked like you could shoot the movie Ants on my kitchen floor. And, my mailman asked me to go out to dinner and a Jazz club with him.

DATING WITH KIDS

One of the best things in life is being a mom, but being a mom trying to find love is terrifying and frustrating. This is why it is important to be careful about who you date, because you will end up marrying one of them, and that can lead to children, and, unfortunately, sometimes divorce. No one ever wants to end up a single mom. Watching a young woman go through divorce is almost more painful than seeing one chased by a serial killer. At least she has the chance to escape, or will die quickly. I know that sounds harsh, but living your life with a crazy ex-husband is like being tortured and dying slowly for years. If I can help one woman date smarter, and prevent the pain of a divorce it was worth writing this book.

I know what I'm talking about because I've raised two boys on my own, and let me tell you, it was not easy. But, if you think it's hard finding a good man when you don't have kids, try dating when you have to schedule around babysitter availability, school activities, childhood illnesses, and the exhaustion of raising children alone. It's hard to have anything left for feeling sexy and interesting, and so many men are like kids in that they don't want to feel as though they come second. There are too many single women without children for them to chose from. Our society has become a culture of instant gratification; if a man has to wait and doesn't get satisfied right way, he probably won't stick around.

And the harsh reality is, while most women are more than willing to date men with kids—a man with children is a prime candidate for marriage, especially if he has money—it's not the same for men. Most men would prefer not to date single moms and face the possibility of raising another man's children. It's unfair that the same rules don't apply, but they don't.

You may have to remain single for a long time and watch your ex move on to another relationship. But, it's better to be alone than to stay with a man who has lied and/or cheated on you or end up in yet another bad relationship. You may not have a man, but you have your pride. It may feel hopeless right now, but single mothers do find happiness, and you can too. Just be patient and don't compromise in what you know is best. As you get older and talk to your married friends about their bad relationships, you will realize that being single isn't bad at all. Hobbies, wine, and good friends are better than having a bad or even average man any day.

FIGURING OUT WHAT YOU WANT

My dad always told me that when you're dating you have to be a detective and really take your time to get to know a man.

Find out as much information subtly as you can without getting your emotions involved, and then, when you find out he's a good man, you can give yourself permission to become more emotionally invested. It makes perfect sense, but it's hard to do.

So, what's your type? Do you know if you even have a type? I hate writing lists, but this is one list you need to make—the Top Ten things you must have in a man. It's important to have a visual, and hold yourself accountable for not compromising on those wants and needs in the men you date. Write down ten traits that will make up the man of your dreams. The top five are the most important and the guy you just went out with MUST have them in order to deserve a second date.

Here are some important examples of qualities a man must have. Use this list as inspiration for your own. Take some time to really think about what is important to *you*, pretty Flower. Does he need to be successful, loyal, loving, spiritual, kind, honest, a MENSA member, or have buns of steel or a big penis, etc.?

This is the list I made:
1. *Super Funny* - I would marry Adam Sandler or Jack Black in a minute
2. *Loyal* – There had better be no other lady centers for him.
3. *Thoughtful* - I love small, sweet, meaningful gifts.
4. *Intelligent*- I love to learn and read and want him to value knowledge too.
5. *Really Masculine* – Everyone has their own characteristics they find attractive. I love a strong, masculine, tall guy.
6. *Older/Mature* – I'm not into raising another boy, so I want someone around ten years older than me.
7. *Super Tall* - The Jolly Green Giant turns me on.
8. *Good Family* – If he comes from good people it's a sign

he will be too!
9. *Understand Love* – He has to have morals and values.
10. *Spiritual* - I need a guy who will go to the Agape Transformation Center with me.

Yup, I'm going to ask you to make another damned list. This time I want you to write down what didn't work in the past. It's really good to look at it on paper and recognize your patterns so you don't repeat them in the future. Ask yourself questions like these:

1. *Was he cheap?* If the last flower you got was one you took off the casket at your aunt's funeral, the answer is yes.
2. *Was he always late?* If you ever passed out from low blood sugar because he was two hours late for dinner, then he definitely had an issue with respecting your time.
3. *Did he lie to you?* If you ever felt like you were dating Pinocchio, unless, for some strange reason you think long noses are sexy, you know you had a bad guy.
4. *Did he ever cheat on you?* If his definition of monogamy was not sleeping with more than one woman a night, it's clear you were not on the same page.
5. *Did he fail on the basic gentlemanly behaviors—opening doors, pulling out chairs, etc.?* If he was more courteous to the guy who details his car, his priorities were not with you.
6. *Was the sex bad or average?* If his penis was smaller than your travel-size vibrator, you are better off with the vibrator.
7. *Did he lack ambition?* If he had a PlayStation 1 through 6 and was saving up for the new one, that isn't the kind of aspiration that matters.
8. *Was he lazy?* If you had to vacuum around him in his recliner after a poker night with his buddies, you were doing way too much work in every area of the

relationship.
9. *Did he drink a lot?* If he visited Happy Hour before picking up your kids from school, he had a problem.
10. *Did he watch too many sports on TV?* If he even watched flag football (Who watches flag football anyway?!) on Saturdays instead of spending time with you and the family, he wasn't focused on the right things.

Or, maybe he was just a dick in general. Whatever your ex did that didn't work for you must no longer be acceptable. Use these lists to learn your lesson, grow, and get ready to play the game of love again.

We all have a type, so don't listen to people who tell you to date out of your type. It's one thing to make the choice to stay away from men like your ex because you already know that didn't work for you. And it is good to keep an open mind so you can get to know people, but don't compromise what you like, and definitely don't compromise on those must-have character traits—especially, if it's going to be your second chance at love. Get exactly what you want or learn to be happy alone. It's important to be able to be by yourself and be okay, pretty Flower! It will make you stronger in a relationship.

When your miserably married friends tell you you're too picky and you need to settle, simply tell them in a loving and sensitive way that you would rather masturbate and be alone the rest of your life than be with someone like their husband, and then ask them not to bring it up again.

You may think you are safe in the big, scary world of dating, but if you are out there under the influence of any kind of distraction or insecurity, you are starting out at a significant disadvantage, and all the crazy killers out there will eat you alive. Okay, maybe not eat you alive, but the damage they can inflict on your mental, emotional, and even physical health will feel as bad.

CHAPTER THREE
"You Have Been Warned"
—*The Omen*

Separating the Boys from the Men

Nothing separates the boys from the men like a crisis. A horror movie will reveal a guy's true nature really quickly. Does he run or does he stay and fight? Does he cower in fear or charge boldly into danger? The ritual of dating can be a real freak show and a major headache to endure, but it definitely is a great test to show you what you are working with.

I've realized one of the problems is women don't know what they deserve, and settle for a boy instead of a man. Big difference. You may hate the game of dating, but don't you want to give yourself time to weed out the guys who aren't ready? Pretty Flower, why would you settle for someone who isn't treating you like butter? It's not okay to take shit from a man because you think it's the best you can do, especially if this is your second chance at love.

Are You Dating a Man or a Boy?
Through all my research I've learned that some people don't really know what a truly healthy relationship looks like—how men should treat women and how women should treat men—and people don't always agree on what that means.

Don't Go in that Room!

Here are some clues:
1. *A man will tell you he loves you all the time.* He won't leave you to be the only one saying it. *A boy thinks you should already know how he feels.* He will assume he doesn't need to say it.
2. *A man will make sure you have no doubts about the relationship.* He will make sure trust is established to set a healthy foundation. *A boy will make you feel insecure and not sure where the relationship stands.* He probably doesn't think about your relationship because he's busy spending more time at work or with his friends than with you.
3. *A man will make you feel like a pretty Flower.* He will tell you with words and actions that you're a beautiful desirable woman. *A boy only gives compliments when you're looking sexy.* He doesn't value your inner beauty.
4. *A man will never lead you on.* He will be willing to talk about commitment and marriage without being vague and evasive. He will tell the world that you're his woman! *A boy will be uncertain about what he wants.* The word marriage will *never* come out of his mouth, and he probably will introduce you by just your name, refusing to say "girlfriend."
5. *A man will work on himself and the relationship.* He understands that he needs to grow emotionally and work at making the relationship the best it can possibly be. *A boy will not work on himself;* he certainly won't be growing emotionally. He thinks that relationships should just work out easily, no effort required on his part.
6. *A man will never lie to you, even if the truth hurts.* He will know how to be sensitive to your feelings and still be honest. *A boy will lie to you, especially if it's easier for him.* And, remember: lies of omission are still lies!
7. *A man will remove himself from dating websites as*

soon as the relationship gets serious. (A man didn't want to be on websites in the first place.) *A boy will keep trolling dating websites.* At most, he will hide his profile, to make sure he isn't missing something better.

8. *A man will never leave you when situations get rocky.* He will do everything in his power to work it out in a mature fashion because he knows what love is. *A boy will leave at the first sign of trouble.* He won't try to work it out at all because he only thinks about himself and doesn't know what love is.
9. *A man will take responsibility for you.* He knows you're a package deal if you have children and will want to be involved in their lives. *A boy will not want responsibility and commitment.* He certainly won't want anything to do with your children.
10. *A man will never tell you he loves you and leave you.* If he says it, he means it and is there to stay. *A boy will use the word "love" as a key to gain access to your lady center.* You can count on him to bail when he gets what he wants.

So, now you have a good idea about whether you're dating a man or a boy, you will have to decide if you're going to be a woman or a girl. Will you stay and let him continue to treat you badly, or will you stand up for yourself and put an end to the bad relationship?

Dana

Dana was an attractive woman, working two jobs while starting her own company and raising her son alone. She was dating a successful, attractive older man, but the relationship was always a bit off. She couldn't exactly put her finger on the problem. He was loving and attentive at the beginning of their courtship. He didn't push her for sex, and their chemistry was off the charts! He sent her small gifts, made nice plans for them, and even took her to his cousin's three-day wedding celebration in Santa Barbara.

He still saw her every weekend, wanted sex with her, texted her every day, and called her every day, so you might wonder what she had to complain about. But, as time went by she saw small signs of disrespect—his words and actions didn't always match up, he stopped saying "I love you" and making plans in advance. One night they were walking back to his house from a lovely dinner when a woman who seemed very upset said "Hi" to him in a very sarcastic way. He barely acknowledged her, and they just kept walking. She asked him who this woman was, and he blew it off as one of the moms at school. The whole thing seemed really odd, and her intuition was going off like sirens from a fire engine, but he was doing all the right things, so she felt crazy for worrying.

Eventually things started to change. She'd break up with him, and did this a few times, only to get back together. She finally sat him down for the "Come to Jesus" talk to see what was up. He said he didn't say "I love you" anymore because he thought it made it less special if he said it all the time. He didn't make plans in advance anymore because they'd been dating for a while. He made excuse after excuse for why all the little things that had made him stand out as a great guy were disappearing.

She didn't want to hire a Private Investigator in case she was wrong and really didn't think he was the type to be cheating and lying. So, I called in my psychic who told her, in detail, about all the women he had been cheating with and all the dating sites he'd been on. It seemed hard to believe, but it prompted her to take it to the next level and contact a PI who confirmed everything the psychic had told her.

A good man won't string a woman along for a year and a half with lies. A good man will be honest about wanting to see other women, or break-up with her. He won't use her for sex while waiting to see what other woman might come along. These are the actions of a boy who isn't ready for relationship responsibility. FYI . . . this guy was fifty-two years-old, so if you are expecting your boy to turn into man by the time he's forty, you may be setting yourself up for major disappointment. Unfortunately, some boys will never grow up.

She took a while to figure out she was dating a boy and a little longer to decide she was going to be a woman and stop taking his abuse of her time and her heart. Don't settle for less than you deserve for a minute longer than it takes him to dish it out that first time.

Ladies, if you're dating a boy and you're aware of it; it's your fault when he hurts you. You're a flower; you don't have time for this behavior. If you choose to stay with a man who treats you poorly in any way or doesn't meet your needs, you can't blame him or be the victim when he leaves you or hurts you.

I know it's hard; I know it hurts, I know it sucks, but it's what dating is. You have to be strong as fuck to date.

Men to Look Out For

As observers, we often see the signs of danger lurking around the bend in horror films. We don't always see those same signs in our dating lives. A lot of times we end up like our girl wandering down a dark street at night, not realizing the psycho killer is hiding in the shadows.

I want you to pay close attention now and study these types of guys you need to watch out for. Avoid them at all costs—including having to sit at home on date night because you passed on their invitation.

BBD

The Bigger Better Deal guy has the mentality that there is a better woman online if he just keeps looking. His thought process goes a little something like this:

This woman is great, but I still think I can get one with D-sized breasts and who is about an inch taller, but not more than an inch.

My last girlfriend was a Dallas Cowboy cheerleader, but I think I can get a Playboy bunny.

I like her a lot; she's everything I want . . . except, maybe I'd like a petite blonde.

You may have great dates with them, but about the time you think it's going really well, you'll find out he's still looking for others to have great dates with. The reality is, he's not ready for a relationship and is usually the really shallow type of man you don't want to date anyway.

What is at the core of it? It's driven by a combination of an oversized ego and an oversized need for self-protection. He is afraid to commit, but he is horribly afraid of rejection too.

It's certainly human nature to make sure you're always getting the best deal, but where does this behavior end and what are the areas that are off-limits for this type of approach? I think it's pretty obvious that we should draw the line where people's hearts are involved. And the BBD guy is only going to change when he gets his ego in check and gets sick of chasing waterfalls. You can't thrive repeating this behavior forever and will end up alone.

There was a time when we could meet someone through a friend, at work, or in our neighborhood who made us happy and we didn't feel we were settling. The internet has a lot of good things to offer, including opening up the dating pool for people who don't like to go to bars or who have a small social circle. The problem is that, along with how we worship celebrities and the "perfect" image they have to maintain, online dating has created the misconception that if we just keep looking we are sure to find the ideal person who checks off every box.

If you find a guy who treats you well and turns you on, you've got what you need and everything else is gravy, so don't be a glutton. If we start doing this ourselves, the BBD guys will be forced to stop shopping around when they have a great woman willing to do the same.

THE PLAYER

The player—he's the tall, strikingly good-looking, super successful man you can just tell has a huge penis and knows how to use it. He has the confidence and charisma you can feel when he walks by.

Everyone knows he's a player, but your lady center doesn't care at all. One small glance from him and you can feel yourself melting like a snowman in the midday sun. You want and need a piece of it. You are fully aware that right after he fucks you he will fuck you over, but you are willing to risk it all for one night with him.

I can't tell you not to go for him if all you really want is a good romp to feed those urges that do come up, but I just want to warn you that you are fooling yourself if you think this is a one-and-done kind of situation. He's like potato chips—you don't ever just eat one and the greasy, salty residue gets all over you. (See the previous chapter on sex and dating again if you forgot why this is true.)

But, he's not the worst type of man at all, pretty Flower!

THE WOLF IN SHEEP'S CLOTHING

The worst type of man is the one who seems so sweet he would never hurt you. He's the man who is probably average in looks and intelligence. He may be short, bald, or have some physical feature that women sometimes find undesirable.

He doesn't treat you like a queen, but doesn't treat you poorly either. The sex is okay, but not particularly passionate, and sometimes you wonder if you're settling. You stay because

Don't Go in that Room!

he meets a lot of your needs and seems like a good man. He's the one your married friends will encourage you to accept. They'll tell you you're being too picky for holding out.

He's gentle and doesn't fit the player profile at all. You don't think he would cheat on you in a million years because he's not what people would really call "a catch," and knows he probably won't do much better than you. He seems like a stand-up guy, but you do wonder sometimes because something is a little off. Your intuition senses something, but you ignore it because you think it's wrong. Then you find out he's just as shady as the player; it's just that the player doesn't try to hide who he is.

It's real, it's shocking, and it's one of the reasons you really need to pay attention to all of the signs a man is giving you. Men show you who they are all the time. This is one big reason you can't drink a lot when you're dating. Your intuition is dulled when you consume alcohol, and you can make the wrong judgment about a man.

Wolves know how to play the game—they know what to do and say to get you to lower your guard and invite them in. When you get blindsided by a wolf in sheep's clothing it can knock the wind out of you and take a long time to heal. The player you will see coming; the sheep you don't detect until it's too late.

James
James had been sleeping with a girl on Saturday nights for the last three months. I asked him if he really liked her and he laughed at me. He told me she called him and texted him during the week and gave him her lady center on Saturdays. He brought take out once, but other than that, she made dinner for him and bought the wine.

He was also having sex with another woman on Tuesdays and a third woman on Thursdays. He told Ms. Saturday he was super busy during the week with work and went to the gym late every night. He had other excuses for Ms. Tuesday and Ms. Thursday.

Ms. Saturday is an example of a woman with low self-esteem who was chasing after a man, doing all the heavy lifting for him. When a man likes you, he initiates contact with you and not just for a booty call. What he was doing was a "dick-ish" move, but you teach people how to treat you. She taught him her lady center came free with dinner thrown in as a bonus. No coupon required.

Most men will tell you what they think you want to hear (or what you've told them you want to hear)—how special you are, how great you are, how no one has made him feel the way he does when he's with you, how he wants to get married someday.

NOTE: He didn't say he wanted to marry you! Men tell me that women read what we want to hear into things they say all the time. They can say vague or even leading things and we just take that ball and run all the way to the end zone with it, not bothering to look back and see if he is coming along with us. This is why we must take time to get to know a man's character before we let him into our lady centers or into our hearts.

Starting Early

Whether you have children, hope to have them someday, have brothers or nephews, or just have influence over someone's life, it is your duty to do your part in helping to get our men back.

If you are a parent, are you teaching your son to become a man? If not, shame on you! You can help end this crazy cycle of men using women for sexual purposes and not treating them with respect. I think we should raise all little boys to think that their penises will fall off if they sleep with a woman they don't love or if they use a woman for sex.

Don't Go in that Room!

This way, even when they learn the truth, it will still always be in the back of their minds, haunting them when they are about to do something selfish and hurtful. Okay, maybe we shouldn't say "fall off," but throwing a little white lie at them to drive home the importance of sexual respect won't hurt.

We should at least teach men about how sex affects women. Did you know that it affects a woman's oxytocin, which lowers her defenses and causes her to trust her sexual partner? Sex is how a woman bonds to a man, and when she lets down her guard, she is more likely to fall in love. Let's get it ingrained in both of the heads men consult that there is a Golden Rule to sex and women that they must live by: They must respect a woman and treat her how they would want someone to treat their mom, sister, or daughter. If they are not acting like the kind of man they would want the women they love to be involved with, then their behavior is not acceptable and they need to change immediately.

Now, let's turn to our daughters. Are you teaching your girl to be a woman? I hope you're teaching the young woman in your life the power and value of her lady center. She needs to know that her emotional and relationship needs must be met for three months before she gives her lady center to a man. You need to teach her that when she has sex, chemicals released from her brain can create confusion about whether a guy is a good one or a bad one, and she can get attached to the wrong man. You must tell her about STDs and pregnancy. The sexual risk for a female is so much greater than for a male. Both of these things have the ability to ruin her life.

Finally, instill in her a strong sense of self and cultivate her self-esteem. Let her know how amazing she is and that she should be valued as a person above all else. The first few boyfriends a girl has can really shape the way she perceives herself and relationships. If she's fully prepared, she stands a fighting chance in this crazy game of love.

Chapter Three

OUR SCHOOLS' RESPONSIBILITY
My son told me he learned to put a condom on a banana at school during Sex Ed. Now, I'm all for teaching proper contraception, but they didn't teach him that before you put that condom on your penis you should have love and respect for the girl you are about to have sex with and understand that sex is different for girls than it is for boys.

Our schools are teaching boys to not get a girl pregnant or pass around diseases, but they are not teaching them to be men who behave with dignity and honor regarding sexual conduct. Is it the schools job to do that? Yes, as a matter of fact, it is. If they are going to show them how to use condoms for sex, then they need to address the psychological impact of sex as well as the physiological aspects.

Our boys are growing up seeing movies that make it cool to use and sleep with a woman, and many aren't getting any correction from family members, mentors, or community leaders. Sex still isn't really brought up freely in many homes, so kids learn from their friends, which is the least effective way to get the right lessons.

I've taught my boys to respect women and that using a woman for sex or cheating on someone you're committed to is just not acceptable. I've raised my boys to open doors for a woman, let a woman off the elevator first, show them love and affection, and to be attentive to their wants and needs, but I've also thrown in that you don't ever let a woman use and abuse you. Please teach your boys to be men, it's your responsibility.

Handling Sex and Relationships with Maturity

So, you have a few flaws; doesn't everyone else? Don't let that be your excuse for settling! If you think you don't deserve a good MAN because you have some flaws, then you shouldn't be dating at all. You should be focusing on self-care.

Don't Go in that Room!

I don't care if you have small breasts, big thighs, are overweight, are too skinny, ugly, didn't go to college, work at a bad or low-paying job, don't have a lot of money, have kids at home, etc. It doesn't matter! You are perfect the way you are and a good man is going to love you. He's looking for YOU. He wants YOU.

I know I'm extremely direct and have a poor choice of words sometimes, but I believe that God is a fair fucking guy and designed you to be you, just the way you are. He also made a man who will love you and all of your perfect imperfections.

Always remember, nobody is perfect and people who pretend they are annoy the rest of us. In fact, the reason I usually like people is because of their flaws and weirdness! Don't you?

PART II
"Just When You Thought it Was Safe
to Go Back Into the Water"
—*Jaws 2*

Finding Your Way Out of the Woods

CHAPTER FOUR
"It's Only a Movie ... It's Only a Movie"
—*The Last House on the Left*

You Are in Control

Let me ask you something. Do you care about you first? Do you take good care of yourself and your happiness before anyone else's happiness? If so, great! You can put down this book and walk away. You don't need me because you're ready to date. But . . . maybe you aren't as ready as you think. Why don't you keep reading just to be sure?

Caring about yourself and your happiness before anyone else's is important. You have to be the love of your own life because you have to live with you for the rest of your life. Self-love is taking care of you first and making sure your needs are met so that relationship is as strong as it can be. Romantic relationships will come and go; if you don't love you first and take care of yourself first, you're not ready to date yet. If you have some self-love to find, it's all good. Find it, and then start dating. You don't want to attract someone who is not good for you.

Like attracts like, so, if you truly love you, you will attract a kind love man who loves himself and you will have a kind, loving relationship based on love and respect for each other.

I had a beautiful older woman come to me about a man who

lived a few houses down the street from her. He had been texting her for the last four months. She was in Cyber Love. She knew he had a girlfriend of two years and said he was going to break-up with the woman but felt bad because she was having some medical issues.

This beautiful woman kept telling me over and over what a good man he was, and I had to point out that a good man wouldn't be texting and calling another woman while he was in a committed relationship. This is cheating, no two-ways about it. I asked her if she were the one having medical issues, and her boyfriend of two years had been texting and calling another woman, how she would feel? When we really like someone it's hard to see something that is painfully obvious.

You can rest assured, if he is willing to cheat in his existing relationship, he will cheat when he's in one with you. I don't care if it's not physical cheating, it's emotional cheating. This great guy is not so great.

A woman who really loves herself would never consider being the other woman. You don't give men their cake and a fork to eat it with too. Walk away from this kind of relationship; in fact, run if you don't have on stilettos.

There are a number of things that affect our ability to love ourselves. It might be that we lack the confidence in ourselves and our abilities, don't value ourselves, or don't think we deserve to ever come first.

Self-Confidence

It is totally normal for your self-confidence to come and go once in a while. We all struggle with feeling self-assured and remembering all of our own great qualities. How often do you look around the room and feel less than everyone else? If you are doing that often, it might be helpful to sit down and write out all the traits you have that you feel good about or that other people have complimented in the past. Take a personal inventory and remind yourself regularly that you have a lot to offer, even if you feel it doesn't measure up to someone else because the truth is, everyone has flaws that make them insecure. They just might be better at covering up how they feel about them.

BALANCING THE SCALES
If you're on a date and you find yourself thinking he is better looking or smarter than you in anyway, fearing he won't want to go out with you again, your self-confidence needs a little work. It's easy to fall into the trap of feeling undeserving, so try this exercise while you're on your date to help boost your confidence: Pretend he has something majorly wrong with him and that you're never going to see him again. This can actually be amusing and make you realize he isn't better than you at all.

1. *Tell yourself he has a penis under two inches.* There is no way in hell he is touching your lady center.
2. *Imagine he has narcolepsy.* OMG, is he sleeping? Is that drool?
3. *Give him some really bad life choices.* Maybe he has a tattoo of the Golden Girls on his left bicep?
4. *Picture him dancing like Elaine on* Seinfeld. With those thumbs and jerky movements, there's no way you could take him to a wedding!
5. *Visualize him dressed for bed like a Power Ranger.* Go, Go Power Rangers!
6. *Maybe he's gay!* He's wearing Prada and he knows you have a Michael Kors bag. If he's just a friend, you can totally relax.
7. *Picture his nose hair growing and growing and growing.* Okay, maybe not; it could make you lose your appetite, and you should be able to enjoy your dinner.

> 8. *Guess what other quirks he has.* Maybe he's obsessed with karaoke. He dresses up like Psy and will only sing "Gangnam Style." *Eh-sexy lady.*

I can do this all day! Make up something really stupid so you don't feel less than; it works like butter! This man has flaws and insecurities too; you just don't know what they are yet. Believe me, he's probably worried you think he's not smart enough, good-looking enough, or you want a younger guy.

He might be sitting there thinking you're too good for him. You don't know what's going on behind his façade. This man is not special, he is human and he is flawed just like you, pretty Flower. I mean, let's be real; even Prince Charming was not perfect—the truth is he probably wore man-Spanx.

Self-Esteem/Self-Worth

Do you know your value as a person? I hope you know how great you are, honor your feelings and needs, believe in your abilities and judgment, respect for yourself and your body, and trust your intuition for making good, loving decisions that are best for you. After all, there is no one on the planet who knows what is best for your life better than you do. Only you know what is right or wrong for you.

Learn to listen to the inner voice that reminds you what you are worth and what you deserve in dating and relationships. Let it help you through the things that can challenge your sense of self-worth, like rejection and disappointment.

REJECTION
There can be a million different reasons a man decides not to ask you out or chooses not to ask for a second date, so don't ever take it personally; you reject people as well for different reasons. It could be he decided you weren't right for

him because you have a dog or cat, like the beach, don't ski, or who the hell knows; just don't take it as an indication that there is something essentially wrong with you.

If you're worried about being rejected, maybe you shouldn't be dating. It is important to understand and accept that not everyone is going to like you, and you are not going to like everyone. Finding the right person who matches up with you is not easy! So many things have to be right for a good relationship to work, it's amazing people actually find each other.

If you go on a few dates and you feel rejected or not good enough STOP dating and work on yourself for another few months. Your emotions will let you know where you are during the dating process; if dating doesn't make you feel good, don't do it.

Carol
Take a lesson from Carol. She went on a coffee date with a man she met online. They had emailed back and forth a few times, but never actually spoke. When they finally decided to meet in person, she was excited by the possibilities, but a little nervous about how he would match up to her expectations and whether she would meet his. As she sat down at the table he looked at her and said with a *severe* stutter, "Yooouuuurrrr, yoo, your, nooootttt, nononontttt, pr prprp pr pr pr pretty eeennnnufff forrrrrrrrrrrr, for me."

Can you imagine going on this date with low self-esteem? I have a motto that helps keep this in perspective: "Rejection is protection."

As all dating women know, most men think they're the prize in the box of Crackerjacks, but most are the popcorn, not even the rare candy-coated peanut. If you don't know that you're the prize, don't date until you are sure you are just as heavenly!

I have friends who look like Barbie dolls and are

lawyers and doctors who get rejected all the time. When rejection comes, you have to remember that, for whatever reason, you're just not the right fit for that man. Be thankful he's a decent enough man that he didn't string you along while he's looking for someone else.

Self-Centering

A woman chased by a clown with a knife shouldn't be concerned about the clown's needs, and a woman being chased by a man with a penis shouldn't be concerned about the man's needs.

In case you didn't know it, you should be preoccupied with how you feel in a relationship. Being self-centered is usually considered a bad thing, but in relationships it's not. Women need to be way more self-centered in relationships than they tend to be. They need to take care of themselves in the relationship more than they take care of their man.

Obsessing about what he's doing, wanting, or thinking is not healthy for you. It only matters what you are doing, wanting, and thinking. Stay focused on you. Focusing on making sure you take care of yourself first ensures that you are strong, secure, and equipped to love him better because you are not cheating yourself out of what you need.

It is very easy to allow yourself to cave to the needs of others, tell yourself that you aren't enough, and convince yourself that you can't date successfully and find lasting love. Don't buy into those false and harmful messages, pretty Flower! You are in control of your dating life and future. Use your power for your good.

CHAPTER FIVE
"When the Lights Go Out the Terror Begins"
—*Alone in the Dark*

The Smart Rules for Sex and Dating

We all know what happens when the lights dim. If you're in a romantic comedy, you and your guy share that steamy kiss and something magical happens. But, in a horror film, when it gets dark, things go horribly awry and someone ends up hurt . . . or worse. This is when the ax-wielding murderers, vampires, and evil spirits are most active. And, when characters are distracted by sex or sexual attraction, they don't get to experience magic, they end up with disaster. In real life, if you allow yourself to be distracted by sexual desire too early in the game, you are going to end up with disaster too.

Part of what makes dating and relationships so terrifying is not knowing what to do when it comes to sex. If you're ready for this chapter, then, *Congratulations!* You're dating someone who could be your Prince Charming and would like to give him your lady center! But, when is the right time to have sex?

It really depends on what you want. If you want him to think of you as nothing more than a way to scratch an itch, sleep with him on the first date. It doesn't matter if this is your first time being "easy," if you sleep with a man on the first date, he will think you've done it a million times. Guys tell me all the time that they think the women who say, "I've never done this before," are full of shit.

If you want him to think of you as a possible wife, don't sleep with him until after he's proven to you that he's a good man. A good man's wife values her lady center and doesn't sleep around.

My 4-foot, 80-lb. Italian grandma used to say to me before she died, "Why would he buy the cow when the milk is free?" It's an old proverb about how men aren't going to make a commitment to you if you are giving away sex so openly. If I ever started giving my lady center away for free, my dead Italian grandma's ghost would haunt me!

Think I'm wrong and that this is just an old-fashioned practice? Want to tell me I'm being prudish and it doesn't work this way in the modern era? Well, let me make my case, and we'll see if you still want to proceed without caution into those dark, scary woods when I'm done.

First-Date Sex

Would you wander down a dark alley with a stranger and expect everything to be okay? Well, think about this: SEX ON A FIRST DATE IS SEX WITH A STRANGER! If you are on the first date (actually dates 1-5), he really doesn't know you. He just knows that you are *hot* and fuckable. He has no loyalty to you whatsoever. Want to guess how I know? Ask yourself, if you turned him down and another girl walked by and offered him sex, would he leave with her or continue his evening with you? If you have to wonder for even a second about whether you can get an Über home, you know he is not deserving of your lady center yet (if ever.)

Besides, sex on the first date might be fulfilling for the night, but it rarely leads to anything meaningful long-term. And what if something goes wrong—he cums too quickly, his penis is too small, he can't give you an orgasm? Then you've wasted an evening and given up something that should be special to you.

Give yourself what you deserve and give the new romance a chance to become something worth having.

Tiffany
Tiffany was a beautiful woman in her late thirties who came to me wondering why she rarely got second dates. She told me that her first dates usually went well and they seemed to have a connection, but they men wouldn't call again or would avoid her calls after that night. I asked her a little more about what happened on the dates and she revealed to me that she was in the habit of giving men access to her lady center on first dates.

My question was, "WTF are you having sex on a first date for if you want a second date?" Poor Flower, she didn't know the value of her lady center and thought it should be free. I explained to her that if you think your lady center is no more valuable than that, then you will be treated like it's a throw-away, you'll be treated like you are disposable.

If you want love, you must require love for the privilege of getting to your lady center. If you want commitment, you must expect commitment before handing over the keys to the kingdom.

30th-Date Sex

We all know the ones who survive to the end of the scary movies are the ones who don't make reckless choices and take a moment to assess the situation before diving in. Deciding you are ready to have sex in a dating relationship is one of those moments when you need to find a place where you can catch your breath and wait until it's safe to come out of hiding. If you are on date thirty, odds are pretty good he knows who you are, and he has continued to show up and spend time with you because he wants you. The relationship has had time to evolve, and you can feel more confident that if you turned him down this time and another woman came along, offering him sex, he would send her on her way because he is invested in you and how he feels about you.

This doesn't mean you have to give him your lady center at this stage. You still may not be ready to go there for whatever reasons. Maybe you've been on thirty dates, but they were all crammed into a month because you saw each other every night. While that's a lot of time together, it still isn't a lot of time in the grand scheme of things, so giving it a little longer is totally reasonable.

It could be your thirty dates have been spread out over a year because one or both of you travel a lot or are really busy and you hardly have time to get together. That is a lot more time on the calendar, but it doesn't guarantee a lot of time really getting to know each other.

The bottom line is you don't have to give up your lady center before you feel it's right; but, when you do, you should make sure you feel he's going to stick around after he gets the goods.

WONDER WOMAN
I never understood why my dad watched Wonder Woman until I got older—Lynda Carter has an amazing figure. When you're dating, you have that same allure; but, as soon as you have sex, you become Diana Prince, who is much more everyday and plain. Wonder Woman oozes with sexy mystery because she seems unattainable.

Men like the chase and having to work to get the lady center. Giving in too soon makes you appear less special. It's just like anything else in life—the things that come easy mean less than the things we have to work hard to earn. We never forget what was on that test we studied for all night long, but don't remember a thing about the ones we breezed through. I bet you get more excited about the last ten pounds you lose than the first ten because they are harder to shed. Expecting your man to put in the work isn't just for you. They benefit from it as well. It makes them appreciate what they finally get.

Engagement or Wedding Night-Sex

There is the rare person in horror films who comes through the whole thing virtually unscathed. They are the ones who didn't open scary-looking doors out of curiosity or run blindly into the woods. They were careful and paid attention to their surroundings so they could respond appropriately.

Now, I'm going to suggest a crazy dating concept in the 21st Century that might get you to the finish line without too many wounds! Wait until you've got the full commitment! Make him put a ring on it first. I know one girl who is waiting until she gets married to have sex. FYI, she's thirty-five. When she tells people about her intentions, they are in absolute shock. They judge her like something is wrong with her.

Respecting your body and wanting love with sex shouldn't be shocking, but more people find it odd to choose not to sleep with a stranger on the first date. That's really pretty sad. What happened to love? Everyone knows sex with someone you really love is amazing, and you can't compare it to getting banged on a first date.

In most cases, women who give into sex before they are ready are doing so because of low self-esteem; they fear he will move on to someone else if they don't give him their lady centers. That's so heartbreaking. If a man is truly interested in you, he is going to be just as willing to give the courtship a chance and see what kind of potential you have. And, as the relationship grows, if he loves you, he's not going anywhere and he will wait for sex. If you think you have to have sex with a man to keep him, you should stop dating and get therapy. You're a beautiful flower! Don't let anyone convince you that you have to devalue yourself and what you have to offer to get a man to stay.

When You Think You're Ready

Sticking your head out of your hiding place to see if the danger has passed, after a long night of terror is one of the hardest things for a character in a scary movie. The monster could be lying in wait, letting our girl get comfortable with the calm so she will take a chance. I don't want to scare you, and I'm not going to tell you when you should or shouldn't have sex. But, I do want to give you some things to consider before you make that choice for yourself—some clues to look for to let you know it's safe to come into the water.

It would be great if women would all get together and set up standards that men must follow before they touch our lady centers. The best idea I've come up with so far is this: We all buy stock in diamonds, and then we set up a requirement for men—if they want to play with our lady centers, we must have an engagement ring. If they screw us over or break-up with us, we can sell the diamond and get the therapy we need to get over the break-up, have one of my fabulous Eulogy parties for closure, and continue making money from our investment in diamonds. Sounds like a great plan to me! We need to somehow catch up on that twenty-two cents pay difference we are screwed out of anyway. I think this would do it!

I'm only partially joking with that. I do think we, at least, should follow these standards for relationships with the good men who want love and commitment. Let's bring some good, old-fashioned courtship back to dating! Let's expect the boys to grow up to be men again! In fact, let's insist on it.

Chapter Five

THE 7 RULES
1. *He must date you for three months and act like a gentleman.* It takes about three months to figure out if you're with a good man and if he's in the relationship for love and commitment. A man won't stick around for three months without sex if he's a player.
2. *He must buy you a substantial gift.* If a man buys you a large gift, he's spending his hard-earned money on you. You know a man won't spend money on a woman he is not serious about. If he isn't treating you like a Flower while you're dating, what type of husband will he be?
3. *He must to take you to places you like.* While you're dating it should be mostly about you, your needs, your wants, your desires, not just his!
4. *He must tell you he loves you or is falling in love with you!* If he isn't thinking in that direction and considering a future and commitment, it is wasting your time and his.
5. *He must introduce you as his girlfriend to his family, friends, and co-workers.* He should be professing to his friends and family that you are this important to him. He should want the world to know.
6. *He must meet your family, friends, and co-workers.* It is important to be able to trust your own intuition about a man, but getting your friends and family's opinions of him to see if they like him is also invaluable. Sometimes they catch things about him you might overlook with your love goggles on.
7. *He must take you on a trip.* Traveling with someone tells you a lot about your compatibility. It also is a great opportunity to finally reward him for all the hard work he's done earning your trust and winning your heart.

Don't Go in that Room!

RELATIONSHIP CONTROL
We all know men need sex, but so do you, pretty Flower. I'm not trying to pretend we aren't sexual creatures as well. But, women tend to approach it differently, and in a way that gets us hurt more easily. That said, did you know you have a secret weapon for protecting yourself during the dark and scary times? You actually hold the real power. Men don't gain any control in your relationship until you give him your lady center.

The truth is, he won't be thinking clearly at the beginning of the relationship because he wants sex. This allows you to teach him how to treat you. Enjoy this time getting to know him and letting him get to know you.

See how he treats you because, once you give him your lady center, he will think he doesn't have to work at earning and deserving you anymore. After sex, you've used up the single dose of your magic potion that makes him moldable, so be sure you have shaped him and the expectations for how you should be treated before you break the seal, so to speak.

It might be really tempting to give up your lady center because you haven't had sex in a long time. I hear ya, Flower! I completely understand. But, it's no different from the discipline you have to use when you are tempted to ruin your diet by that big hunk of chocolatey goodness on the dessert tray. When you are feeling a moment of weakness, grab your girlfriend or gay BFF, head to the sex shop, and pick up a new vibrator. Don't give in and destroy any potential for a good, healthy, committed relationship.

SERIOUSLY, NO JUDGMENT HERE
Listen, I'm not here to judge you if you decide to give free access to your lady center. More power to you! Keep whoring around if sex is all you are looking for. Just remember, if you want to be respected, loved, cherished, and taken seriously to become a man's wife, this kind of behavior won't get you

there.

As I said, I'm not going to judge you if this is how you choose to live your life, but, I would like to ask you to consider how your behavior affects other women who have high standards when it comes to love, relationships, and sex. Also, think about how it will affect you in your future relationships. You may not be looking for commitment now, but that's the kind of reputation that doesn't wash off easily.

Lauren
Lauren is a successful woman who worked for a really large financial company in New York. Over a period of about two years, she slept with four men at her company. Then she got pretty serious with a new man who had just joined the company. One day, while he was in the lunchroom, one of the men Lauren slept with, told her new guy that he'd had sex with her, and so did two other guys in the company. He was super embarrassed that his girlfriend slept with so many men from work.

He really liked her, and they had actually been talking about moving in together, so when he confronted her about the men, he told her he couldn't see her as the really sweet, pretty woman he had been falling in love with anymore, and he ended their relationship. What made it worse was the guy who told him Lauren was sleeping around was a real jerk. A lot of the men in the company didn't like him; he was known as a player, so her sleeping with someone like him lowered his perceived value of her.

Men judge you by who you've dated, married, or slept with, so make your choices wisely. If you've slept with a bunch of players and a good man finds out, you might be screwed.

The thing is, men try to have sex with women on first dates all the time, but they shouldn't think that is even an option with women who want love, a relationship, or marriage. They need to know the difference! And, the solution is simple: if you are going to have sex casually, make sure men understand you don't see them as relationship material. Make sure they get the fact that you are making a purposeful choice to get sex to satisfy yourself. Let them know you don't expect to be called, texted, or taken out on a date ever again by them. They should be clear that you are using them and will go to another man for a relationship that matters. This is called flipping the script. Men don't often get treated the way they treat women—as pieces of meat—and it is a good, harsh reality for them to wake up to sometimes. Just be careful to make sure you really don't want a relationship with them because there is no coming back from this kind of move. You also have to be in a really solid place emotionally to be strong enough to move on and look for what you really deserve.

I do know of a few couples who went on to get married after having sex on their first dates; but, I have to say, they don't have the most healthy relationships. They're not relationships I would want to be in, or that I would want for my friends or anyone I really know and like.

POLTERGEISTS AND OTHER PARASITES
We've gone through the emotional dangers of sleeping around, but we do need to be real about the physical ones as well. Getting up close and intimate with men is all fun and games until someone gets a nasty infection.

You probably had Sex-Ed in health class where you learned about the reproductive system and STDs, but how much thought do you actually give to those things when you are getting hot and heavy? We might think to take care of contraception ahead of time. We might even keep a stock of condoms, but most people end up with nightmare scenarios because they aren't really diligent in this area or don't think about some of the lesser-known problems that can come up.

Chapter Five

Let me share with you a few horror stories:
- A beautiful friend of mine, who was almost past the baby-making years, wanted nothing more than to have a baby. I think she stopped using condoms because she just wanted to get pregnant. She went on a date with someone she met online and slept with him that night. She didn't get pregnant, but she did get Gonorrhea.
- A gay friend of mine had sex on a first date and the condom broke. He ended up with HIV.
- Another friend of mine had sex for the first time at age twenty-six. She wanted to wait for love, but when love didn't happen by the time she was approaching thirty, she said, "Fuck it, I'm just going to go out and have sex." She got sex, but she also got herpes.
- I don't have room to go into all of the women I know who got pregnant by accident through the years, but I do want to share this one: She had a one-night stand and five months later found out she was pregnant. She didn't even know the guy's last name. She'd always had irregular periods and didn't even know if she would be able to have children, so, by the time she realized she was pregnant it was too late for an abortion. It took her two weeks and lots of phone calls to finally track down the guy to let him know.

Most people know about STDs and some even stop to ask if their potential partner is clean, but how many of you think about oral hygiene? Kissing can lead to so much more than just sex! Even if you don't get naked, you can be just as exposed by making out. Here's a list of things you can pick up from what might seem pretty innocent:
- *Colds* – He may not be showing symptoms yet. But, can you afford to take time off work?
- *Mono* – It's called the "Kissing Disease" for a reason! And it can take a long time to get over.

Don't Go in that Room!

- *Herpes* – Herpes is for life, and cold sores are so unattractive!
- *Hepatitis B* – Yep, that's a serious one. I hope you had the vaccination.
- *Tooth Decay* – And you thought it was just from not flossing your own teeth!

These are just a few. There are more to consider, and some can be life-threatening. My friend Jane went on five dates with a very nice, successful man she met online, but it never really felt right, so she ended it, though she felt bad breaking up with him when she did because he wasn't feeling very well on the last two dates.

Before they broke up she had gotten a gag birthday gift for him—the kind that relates to an inside joke that you can't really give to anyone else. She called him to arrange a time to give him the gift but he didn't answer. A week later she called him again to see if she could drop it off and he didn't answer. She gave up and figured he was upset about the break-up.

A week later he called her and told her he had been in the hospital with meningitis. Meningitis is highly contagious and can be fatal. Jane was beyond lucky she didn't contract it. She didn't online date for a long time!

Finally, sex isn't just a physical experience, it's a spiritual one. When you have sex, your aura, mind, and DNA are mixing together. When you have sex with someone on a regular basis over a long period, it can take some time to get rid of this person's spirit that became attached to you during the months or years of intercourse. This is why it's so important to choose your sexual partners wisely and avoid one-night stands.

You may not believe in this stuff, but there is an emotional connection established when two people have sex. This is why one-night stands can be dangerous. People aren't thinking about the energy exchange; they're only thinking about the physical pleasure. You're not only exchanging possible sicknesses and diseases; you also exchange emotions.

On an energetic level, you deposit energy into each other during sex. You're not just connecting with his penis, you're connecting with his spirit, and your body retains the energy of those you have sex with. And negative energy could haunt your lady center for a while. Are you okay with a poltergeist happening all up in your lady center? If you had a one-night stand and you're feeling bad the next day, it might not only be a disease that you picked up. You could've picked up some negative energy and need to get rid of it ASAP.

Getting the Poltergeist Out of Your Lady Center

Follow these instructions immediately if you think you Lady Center has been possessed:
1. Fill the tub with warm water;
2. Add a cup of Epsom Salts;
3. Add a few drops of lavender;
4. Sit in the tub for at least twenty minutes;
5. Get out and pat yourself dry;
6. Burn a ton of sage around you.

That should clear it out, but remember . . . your lady center shouldn't be risking energy attachments!

Let me throw in some quick accidental sex prevention tips. You don't want to miss brunch with your girlfriends the next day because you're busy getting the Poltergeist out of your lady center.

1. *Don't drink alcohol.* I know I'm getting repetitive, but most sexual regrets don't come from decisions made while sober.
2. *Don't ever invite a man in or go to his house on the first*

few dates. Remember, even a small penis is tempting if you haven't had sex in awhile.
3. *Wear jumpsuits.* You're a smart flower; you can figure that one out.

Self-Assessment

So, now that we have gone through all the things you want to avoid, let's take a look at how you can decide for sure you are at the place in your relationship to let the lights go out and feel safe.

Ask yourself these questions and really spend some time thinking about your answers. I'm not going to give you any kind of answer key because this is personal, and what is right for you may not be right for someone else.

It's time to lay it out: What are your lady center requirements?

1. How long do you need to date him and how exclusively?
2. Can he be dating or free to have sex with other people?
3. Do you need love? Do you need to hear, "I love you"?
4. Do you want to get married or be married first?
5. Do you need to have met his family/kids/co-workers/neighbors?
6. Do you require a gift or some indication of his level of investment in you?
7. Do you need flowers and cards or other expressions of affection and thoughtfulness?
8. Do you need a few romantic getaways first?
9. Do you need thoughtful, planned dates?
10. How many thoughtful dates do you need?

If you don't set requirements for sex, you will end up compromising yourself and will feel used and hurt.

Chapter Five

SEXUAL CONCLUSION

We all have to make decisions about sex and dating based on our personal needs and expectations. If you don't want and have no expectations for a relationship, by all means, get your groove on. Just remember that the woman who comes after you is going to be facing an uphill battle getting what she wants and needs if you have distorted his expectations of what women want. Be clear and upfront and give your sister a fighting chance.

I once went on a date with a super attractive, successful, tall man. We were having a great date, so I even went to dinner with him, which I never do. After dinner we were waiting for the valet. He asked me if I have sex on the first date. I didn't answer because I thought the question was inappropriate and I was very insulted. (Remember, not responding is a response.) I think he knew he pissed me off so he proceeded to tell me that he slept with his last two girlfriends on the first date, trying to suggest that if I gave him my lady center we could have a relationship. So, I decided to respond with this: "I only have sex on first dates if the guy's penis is over eight inches." He drove me home.

If you do want a romantic future with the man you are dating, make wise choices about when to take it to that level. Don't cave in because you are afraid you'll lose him or because you've been missing the intimacy you had in the past. Having a man look you in the eyes, tell you he loves you, and kiss you on the head while he holds you after sex is way more fulfilling than someone saying, "Thanks for the sex. It was nice to meet you Jen, I mean Pam," as he's running out the door.

Always remember, when you have sex with someone you are giving them not only your body, you are giving them your dreams of love, your trust that they won't hurt you, your heart, and your health.

CHAPTER SIX
"I Warned You Not to Go Out Tonight"
—*Maniac*

What's Done is Done, But You Can Learn from It

No one likes to hear, "I told you so," but especially not when you are trying to get yourself away from a psychotic killer who has you trapped in a room with no windows at the end of the hallway you knew you shouldn't run to, but ended up in because you panicked.

And the truth is, "I told you so," never helps. How does telling someone you knew they were going to screw up before they did offer anything useful? Other than making yourself feel superior, it is a pointless thing to say.

However, that doesn't mean you shouldn't have someone you trust point out where you went wrong and what you can do differently in the future. Thankfully, in most cases, the bad decisions you make in dating aren't the kind you can't come back from and you will live to screw up another day. But, I'm here to help you avoid making the same mistakes over and over or worse ones.

If you think you are you ready to be asked out, here are a few challenges you might encounter that can set you up for an "I told you so" moment. Learn how to avoid these before you get yourself into a bad situation.

What Do I Say if a Guy Asks Me Out and I'm Not

Interested?

We've been talking a lot about the nightmare scenarios women face in dating, but this is one for the men. It takes courage for a guy to actually go up to a girl and ask her out. I don't think we should ever make men feel rejected. His ego will have less of a blow if he thinks, "She had a boyfriend" instead of "She didn't like *me*," so it might not be unforgivable to tell a white lie to him.

You might tell him you are seeing someone else. You might say you just aren't in a place where you want to date right now. (You do need to be careful with this one in case he says, "Neither do I, I just want to have sex with you." You have every right to be offended, but throw his drink in his face; never ever waste your alcohol. I made that mistake once and had to buy a second $15 dollar glass of Pinot Grigio. Well, the bartender gave me one on the house for having balls, but I almost had to pay.)

Regardless of what you choose, it should be done like a business deal. Be short, direct, and lovely. Remember, you don't ever owe anyone an explanation, and you should always be flattered that someone finds you super cute. You're a fabulous Flower; of course men want to date you!

A single girl should always be prepared to get asked out. You need one response ready for if you like him and one for if you don't like him. If you do like him, please have a Google voice number so you're not giving out your real phone number to a stranger. Make sure you have his full name and Google him before you go out with him. Also, make sure at least one friend knows when you are going out with him and where. Be safe.

HELPFUL HINT: If you are out with your friends and you seriously don't want to be bothered, wear an old engagement ring. If you don't have one, go on Groupon. They have cute fake rings listed all the time.

How Do I Handle Dating More than One Guy?

Juggling the attentions of more than one man is the kind of problem we are more likely to see in a comedy than in a horror film, but if you don't do it well, it can become a disaster. It might be tempting to lie and tell the guy you've just started dating that the reason you can't go out tonight is because you have a family commitment or have to work late. Don't do that; it's what guys do. As women, we should set the right example and tell men straight out, "I have another date." They may not like it, but if they haven't committed to you yet, they should know straight out that you're dating other men and don't have any intention of stopping until they are fully committed to you and ask you not to see anyone else.

Why should you hide the fact that other men want to take you out? And why shouldn't you be allowed to date more than one man at a time? You certainly shouldn't be ashamed of it if you are guarding your heart and your lady center in the process of searching for the right fit.

Is it Ever Okay to Date a Married Man?

If there is one single dating mistake that perfectly represents the "Don't Go in that Room!" mantra of this book, it's dating a married man. I can't stress enough how nightmare-inducing this one choice is for everyone involved. I'm warning you now, this is going to be a long section because it's really personal for me and, while there really is only one answer, there is a lot to say on the subject.

First, from me and all the other women in the world who have been cheated on to all the ladies who think it is okay to mess with someone else's husband, *What the hell is wrong with you? What are you thinking? Don't you have respect for other women, for yourself, and for your lady center?*

Don't Go in that Room!

Obviously, I have a vested interest in this one because I wasn't just cheated on, I actually walked in (with our baby in my arms) to find my ex having sex with someone. And it wasn't just a one-time mistake. He had a bad habit of being unable to keep it in his pants. It's a super long story I will cover more in my next book, which is on divorce. But this still brings up painful memories for me. It took me years to not be traumatized by it, and I still have nightmares sometimes. I make a lot of jokes to cope with the pain—she had really great breasts, she really did. But, I never talk about the fact that I ended up in the hospital on an IV sucking on ice chips because I got dehydrated. (After seeing what I saw I couldn't stop vomiting.) I've always been about 105 lbs., but I lay in that hospital at 94 lbs. I was really sick.

Years after that incident, I got skin cancer on my chest. My western medicine doctor told me it was from the sun, but my Eastern medicine doctor pointed out that if it was from the sun people wouldn't get skin cancer where the sun doesn't shine, and a spiritual healer told me, "Of course you got cancer over your heart; it's broken."

People get really hurt from affairs, and it can destroy families. I know I'll never get back the piece of my heart that incident took from me, but I've learned to live without it. I'm actually thankful for the experience; it made me stronger than I ever knew I could be, and I know in my heart that whatever happens to me in life, it will never hurt me more than I was hurt that night.

Yes, that incident almost killed me, but life is way too short to wallow in that pain, and I have learned that looking for some humor in a situation does a lot to help you cope. So, after I found my husband in bed with another woman I did what any woman would do whose husband cheated on her before the holidays. I sent a Christmas card to the new participant in our relationship. It was a beautiful picture of my son and me. This is what I wrote inside:

Chapter Six

Dear [Woman I won't dignify with a name],

I hope you have a Merry Christmas with your husband and children! I don't have a family to spend Christmas with this year because you fucked my husband.

Much Love and Joy,
Annette Marie

Playing around with people's hearts is not a game. I don't think women who are sleeping with married men take into consideration the wife's feelings, or even worse, the pain they're going to cause their children.

Now, I'm certainly not saying it's all the woman's fault, but I am saying that women need to stick together and not fuck each other's husbands. Men hurt us enough, we don't need to hurt each other.

Unfortunately, a lot of men cheat, but research shows the ladies are starting to catch up. After all, who are men cheating with? Yes, there are men married to women who cheat with men, but usually they cheat with women. We say men are dogs, but we are the ones sleeping with them, allowing this behavior to happen. We have the power to prevent this. Take candy away from a kid, they don't have candy. Take alcohol away from an alcoholic, they don't have alcohol. Take the lady center away from men, they can't have sex. Ya following me?

I am going to give one exception that is completely childish, but hard to criticize. I know a woman whose ex-husband married one of the many girls at work he was having sex with during their marriage. After he remarried, she slept with him one last time as a "fuck you" to his new wife who had been just awful to her. It's wrong and petty, but I understand it! Did she feel good about it after? No, it actually made her feel worse because she sunk to their level and it wasn't who she was.

You may want to find other excuses or justifications for making yourself feel better about sleeping with a married man, but there aren't any. You may say, "But his wife is . . .," and that's a good try, pretty Flower, but it doesn't fly.

I've talked to numerous women who were sleeping with married men. They all told me his wife is a bitch, she's not fulfilling his needs in some way, or he doesn't love her anymore, and they fell in love. I get you, but it's time for a come-to-Jesus meeting.

1. Even if his wife is a bitch, like every other woman at some point in her life, she still doesn't deserve a woman sleeping with her husband.
2. Even if his wife is not fulfilling his needs, there are many options for dealing with this. He can leave her instead of cheating. They can go to therapy and try to work on the marriage, instead of cheating. Men want you to give them their cake and a fork to eat it too.
3. Even if he says he loves you, he is still married. You have to ask yourself, why aren't you his wife yet? Things really aren't as complicated as he needs you to believe. BTW . . . good luck on your marriage to this man if he were to leave his wife for you. He will most likely cheat on you too.

But, you can look at this another way: A women who is willing to sleep with a married man might have done the wife a favor. She helped her get rid of an unfaithful husband. She may have given her a chance to be with a good, loyal man, and maybe saved her from getting herpes too. Always look for ways to turn negatives into positives!

Remember, Karma is a bitch. Every woman I know who had an affair with a married man before they were married ended up being cheated on as well. I know you're going to say, "But I know a guy who didn't cheat on his new wife." Let me tell you, you just don't know about the cheating, or he hasn't had the opportunity for it yet, but it will happen because cheaters cheat. Yes, of course, there are rare cases where a man will stay faithful to a new relationship . . . just as there are very rare Pokémon . . . and Leprechauns.

How Do I Deal With a Guy Who Is Lying to Me?

Encountering lies will come up as surely as a vampire rising from the dead while our girl walks alone through the cemetery in a horror film. If you find yourself wondering, *Is my spouse or boyfriend cheating? Is there something they aren't telling me about their past? Are they keeping something from me about their life?* They probably are. I know that's not what you want to hear. But, the odds are really good that if your Spidey-sense is tingling, there is a good reason for it.

If you are growing suspicious of your man's behavior, don't bury your head in the sand and hope everything works out okay. But, don't confront him without proof. A practiced liar will be able to cover himself and make you feel foolish at the same time, and then all you've done is alert him to the fact that he needs to be more sneaky.

If you really think he's hiding something from you that could affect you and your family and you can afford to, hire a private investigator to look into his actions. If you can't afford one, do research on your own. With social media, email, and smart phones, a liar is bound to leave a trail, and you can find your answers.

Julie
The only reason you should ever put up with a man's lies is for the entertainment value. Julie was dating a guy, and she hadn't seen him for a week because she was busy with work. She finally had a night open, but he told her he couldn't see

Don't Go in that Room!

her Friday night because he was going to the gym and for sushi with his adult son. (He lived with his son and he saw him all week.) The guy she was dating was still on a ton of dating websites even after he told her they were exclusive. He only closed his profile for the one website they met on, thinking she was stupid and wouldn't find out.

There are two possibilities here: 1) He was lying about who he actually was spending time with; or, 2) he really was choosing to spend Friday night with his adult son he saw all the time, and that was a sign he really wasn't interested in her.

Laugh at your man's lies, and when he asks you out next time tell him you are sorry, but you can't go out with him because you are going to the gym and to get sushi with your son (even if you don't have a son or go to the gym and hate sushi.) In fact, repeat the precise lie he told you and see if he catches on.

If you don't want to be that obvious and dish it back at him, make some fun things up. Tell him:

1. I have to wash/condition my hair; deep conditioning is a very important part of my life.
2. I have to spend time with my hamster. I think he's upset—he just keeps running on his wheel. I need to be here for him because he really shouldn't be alone in this fragile state.
3. I need to reorganize my spoon collection. I'm having the girls over for wine tomorrow and someone may possibly need a spoon. Being prepared for what life throws at you is so important.
4. I'm just really wiped out. I had a champagne lunch, massage, facial, and pedicure today. I don't want to go out and get sick.
5. I need to stay home tonight. I have to get up by noon tomorrow to take my grandma shopping. I don't want to be tired. My grandma may be in a wheelchair, but she is super active!

Chapter Six

Is it Okay to Snoop in His Stuff?

You know what they say about curiosity killing the cat. Don't be that girl who is just crazy jealous and creates problems where there are none. In horror movies the ones who go poking around where they shouldn't are the first to die, so before you start going through a man's personal things or hiring a PI, make sure it's not your own insecurities driving you to think he is cheating.

If a man finds out you invaded his privacy this way and he is not cheating, you could lose him for good. Accusing someone of cheating is serious, so you'd better be sure he is giving you good reason for being suspicious before you spend a lot of time and money. Otherwise you could risk losing someone you love because you're just being paranoid.

That said, if you do believe there is reason to worry, I recommend seeking the advice of a psychic to help you decide if your fears are legitimate, and then invest in a PI to get your proof. Psychics get a bad rap because there are some dishonest ones, but you'll find dishonesty in every profession. All the information I received from my psychic about my boyfriends has always been 100% accurate. But, honestly it wasn't anything my intuition didn't already know.

We are all naturally psychic, we just don't know how to use it, or don't want to listen to our feelings. I've taken numerous classes on intuition, and read tons of books on the topic. Developing my intuition has helped me in so many areas of my life. I have learned how to look at someone and get a sense of whether they are telling me the truth. I just didn't want to listen most of the time, or my emotions about the situations were too strong to get the clear picture. When your emotions are involved your intuition comes through like the old dial-up Internet. Remember when you would wait ten minutes to connect with that weird squealing noise?

It's imperative to consult someone during stressful

times because your intuition might not come through clearly. But, never go to someone on the street or to one of those places with the big neon signs. The best psychics usually have a great reputation, have been on TV, or have written a popular book. Unfortunately, they're hard to get in with and are super expensive, although it's pretty much the same as the price of a good therapist, and you might get more clarity this way.

Once you get the info from a psychic, you may not even want to confront your guy if you're just dating; you can just vanish and never talk to him again. If you're married, disappearing is a lot more complicated, so you can just take steps to surprise him with divorce, or you can choose to talk to him about it. I recommend asking him questions and take notes to trap him in his lies. It might make the whole break-up easier for you to hear someone you love lie to your face. It certainly helps bring things into really clear perspective. A person who can look you in the eyes and tell you lies doesn't have the kind of character you want in the man you are spending your life with.

Whether you work on developing your own intuition, consult a psychic, or go a more conservative route and see a counselor, you need perspective to make sure you have legitimate concerns before you go and blow up your relationship with accusations or snooping around in his private business. A good rule of thumb is "Trust, but verify." Give him the benefit of the doubt until he gives you a reason not to.

What Do I Do if I Suspect He Has a Substance Abuse Problem?

I've used the scary movie analogy throughout this book as kind of a joke in a lot of ways, but here is one that is truly scary and can have life-or-death consequences. Dealing with addiction is a really harsh way of life whether you are the addict or in a relationship with one. If you are already invested in a relationship with someone before you realize they have a problem or if it manifests after you are already married, there are a lot of resources to help you cope as a couple and as a family. You may still end up having to walk away, but when there is a marriage or children involved, you may want to hang in there and see if you can get the help necessary to recover.

But, if you are just starting to date and you begin to realize he may have a problem, run quickly in the other direction. Do not pass GO, do not collect $200. Exit the game immediately!

Do not convince yourself you are Bob the Builder and can fix all of his shit. That is no way to start a successful relationship. Just say *no* to men with alcohol or drug problems. Relationships are difficult enough. Sometimes it takes time to find out that they have these problems, but as soon as you do, say, "Bye, Felicia." There is no saving them. They have to do it on their own. You may have a lady center of gold with a DEL (Diamond-Encrusted Labia), but it will never be stronger than the hold their DOC (Drug of Choice) has over them.

If he get's help and some time passes, and if you're still available, he could be a good man, but there will always be a chance of relapse. Only you can decide if you can live with that.

Is it a Good Idea to Try to Change Him?

This is the part of the movie where our girl narrowly escapes the vampire ... or so she thinks. But, as the sun sets, a different "person" emerges and the nightmare begins.

In real life we sometimes take on a work in progress thinking we can change him into something else. We may think we will end up with Boyfriend 2.0 if we just make a few adjustments here and there, but we are more likely to end up with Frankenstein's monster.

If you are telling yourself he may become president someday, even though right now he doesn't even have a job and isn't really looking for one, you are setting yourself up for bitter disappointment. You must take men as they are in the moment. If he's not what you want right now, leave. Sure, it's possible he could become president and you may regret your decision, but it's far more likely he will continue to be a bum and cause you more heartache. Waiting around for him to change could mean you end up with a beast you should have avoided and cost you the true love of your life.

Ladies, the unfair truth is a man is not going to wait for you to have potential. If you're not attractive to him now, he's not going to sit around imagining what you could become. Men are visual and care a lot more about looks than we do. While we do want someone who is attractive, we are more concerned with making sure he can help take care of us and our children. Most men don't care what you do as long as you have a job, but they absolutely do care how big your tuchus is and how large or small your breasts are.

I once found myself in a debate with a man over this issue of potential. He felt that women should wait for men who are trying really hard to get their finances together and become successful. This particular man really liked skinny girls with large breasts and wouldn't give a second look at other types.

I asked him, "What if you meet a really good woman but she is flat chested? She is thinking about getting breast implants someday, but she isn't sure. There is potential that she may have big beautiful D-sized mountains on her chest, but she may stay flat chested. Or, what if you meet a really good woman who is overweight? She is on a diet and she's trying to lose weight, so there is potential that she will be a size 2 in LA and NY (an 8 everywhere else in the world) someday. Do you go out with the overweight girl who's really trying to loose weight?"

He had no response because he knew I'd made my point beyond any argument. You can't make someone turn into the person you want them to be. And you shouldn't want to try. Would you want someone to change you into something you're not?

I pole dance, listen to 80s music, can't cook at all, pass out after two glasses of wine, love nice shoes, and go to bed early. If a man thought he could get me to change things about myself that are unique to me like my pole dancing because he doesn't understand it's a sport, if he wanted me to stop dancing around the house in my Jimmy Choos to Exposé and Stevie B, or expected me to cook for him, he would be in for a rude awakening (and a trip to the emergency room since I *really* have no business in the kitchen). There is no potential here; I've reached my potential. I like me and my life choices.

Take men for who and what they are now. Don't set both of you up for disappointment and failure. If his quirks and limitations aren't something you can live with, he isn't for you, so it's best to move on and find someone closer to your type. I will add one final thing to consider. Make sure that in the process of trying to find your ideal mate that you aren't setting impossibly high standards that no man—no human—could ever meet. It's fine to want a guy with a stable career who makes good money choices and will be a good provider for his family, but to refuse to date anyone with a net worth less than a billion is unrealistic. Write down your list of requirements, and if you find you have just described a creature that doesn't exist in nature, it might be time for a reality check.

Should I Move in with Him?

Should our girl open the door to the basement and go check out the creepy moans coming from the furnace? Yeah, you'll get the same answer that I'd give for whether you should move in with your guy.

You may not like it, but here it is, pretty Flower: If you want marriage, don't move in together until you're married! Studies have shown that people who live together before marriage are less satisfied with their marriages. If you are considering this, please research the "Cohabitation effect."

Marriage is a conscious choice to commit to the person you love for the rest of your life. Living together is what people do when they aren't ready for a commitment but want to spend more time with their partner or can't afford their rent alone. Those who slip into marriage from this type of relationship will most likely end up in divorce because they didn't make the conscious choice to get married. They just did so because it was the logical "next step," even though they probably shouldn't be getting married and probably wouldn't have if they weren't already living together. "In for a penny, in for a pound," is a bad reason to get into a lifetime commitment.

Men tend to be in favor of living with women to test out the relationship. Do you want to audition for someone everyday? Because that's what you are doing, and it will create resentment and bitterness. Why give your heart and body to someone who isn't sure about you? If you don't know the person you're spending time with after dating for a year, having sleepovers, vacations, family outings, and you think living together will help, you're not ready for a marriage.

I did live with my ex in my twenties—I was young and stupid—but, I would never consider it again. He moved in with me because I couldn't afford the rent and he needed a place to live as well. I would never consider it now, especially now that I have children and I'm educated about relationships. We ended up divorced, so that should tell you all you need to know. We were two people who never should have even dated yet ended up married because we lived together. For us, marriage was a forced next step in a relationship that was never meant to be.

I'm not going to judge you if you do move in with your guy if you're in your twenties or don't have any intention of ever getting married. There are an estimated 7.5 million people who live together without being married. But, I certainly hope you moved in together out of love, get married because you truly love that person and want to spend the rest of your life with them, and not out of obligation because it feels inevitable or you just don't want to date again. Dating is hell, but a bad divorce is worse. Trust me on that.

Dating and relationships are full of traps and snares that can put you in a vulnerable position where you are a sitting duck, waiting to be the next victim of a horrific scenario. I hope I've helped you avoid some of the biggest mistakes women tend to make as they venture into the madness of dating life. Always be on the look out for temptations to take the quickest, easiest, or most attractive route to happiness. Those are the ones that usually hold the most hidden dangers.

Now go and date with caution. *You have been warned!*

CHAPTER SEVEN
"Think You're Alone? Think Again"
—*Hollow Man*

You Can't Force it if He Doesn't Like You, Pretty Flower

So, there she is, going about her business, our young woman settling in with her popcorn and a bottle of wine to watch a movie. She hears a sound and the dog starts whimpering and hides under the bed. The house is empty, or so she thought. Something lurks in the shadows threatening to ruin her sense of safety and security. It is a menacing presence that could be the end of her.

You've seen it in the movies, but you may also be experiencing it in your love life. Do you have a nagging feeling that something just isn't right? Are you sensing that something is off? Have your thoughts been sharing their space with an intruder? Well, you might be dealing with the fiendish invasion of a reality check.

If you have been making excuses for why he didn't call, why he cancelled at the last minute, why he's not committing to you, why you're not included in his Facebook pictures, why you haven't met his family or friends, or why he's not giving you the respect you deserve, you know something is off. And, pretty Flower, I hate to say it, but it's usually because he doesn't really like you.

Now, he might be stringing you along because you are a great backup if nothing else works out and you keep letting him get away with not valuing you. He might be keeping you around because he is insecure and needs the validation of knowing someone is there to be his "beck-and-call" girl. We could even give him the benefit of the doubt and consider he might not even realize he's being unfair to you because he enjoys your company but doesn't *really* like you.

Well, none of that matters because this one is on you, Flower. Remember how we talked earlier about teaching men how to treat us? This is where that lesson is really going to come in handy. But, please don't take "I don't like you" personally. It's really unnecessary and a waste of time. Rejection can be the best thing that happened to you. It can make you a stronger woman, make you work harder, learn what type of man to stay away from, and most important, teach you about you. Life is about learning about yourself, and figuring out what is best for you so you can be happy.

Just promise me that if you come to the realization that he is saying, "I don't like you," through his actions you will leave the relationship. You are too valuable to demean yourself by sticking around, begging him to like you. You absolutely can't settle or let a man treat you poorly, especially if this is going to be your second or third husband. Get the good man you want, or be happy alone.

How Will I Know?

As the great Whitney Houston sang, it can be hard to know for sure if he really loves you because sometimes he truly is busy or something happened with his family. But, if he is worth having, he won't leave you hanging in doubt for long.

So, let's look at this chart as a translation guide:

Chapter Seven

What he says/does...	What it means...	What you think...	What you should say/do...
He's too busy.	You aren't important to him.	I wouldn't want a lazy guy who is around all the time.	Okay, bye.
He doesn't return calls or texts.	He's avoiding you.	Maybe he lost his phone.	Okay, bye.
He stops making plans.	He's really not interested.	He'll call when he is free.	Okay, bye.
He won't meet your family.	You aren't important to him.	He's worried they won't like him.	Okay, bye.
He doesn't pay for dinner.	You aren't worth it. He knows he can have you for free.	We are a progressive couple and take turns.	Okay, bye.
He won't call you his girlfriend.	You aren't his girlfriend.	We are a progressive couple and don't need labels.	Okay, bye.
He doesn't want a relationship.	You aren't the one.	He'll come around with more time.	Okay, bye.
He's still seeing other women.	This isn't going anywhere.	He just needs to get this out of his system before he settles down.	Okay, bye.
He isn't interested in sex with you.	He isn't attracted to you.	He's just being respectful.	Okay, bye.
He pushes for sex on the first date.	He doesn't see a future with you.	He's just a normal guy.	Okay, fuck you.

Don't Go in that Room!

This is how it should look, pretty Flower!

What he does ...	What it means ...
He's not too busy to make time for you.	He wants you to be a part of his life because he sees how great you are.
He calls you every day.	He needs to hear your voice every day because you matter to him.
He asks to see you.	He wants to spend time with you because he enjoys being with you.
He texts a lot and often.	He needs to stay connected to you because he wants to make sure you are thinking of him.
He wants to meet your family.	He is serious about your relationship and wants to deepen the connection.
He does things for you voluntarily.	He wants to take care of you because your happiness is important to him.
He plans special dates.	He isn't leaving anything to the last minute and risk not being able to spend time with you.
He introduces you as his girlfriend.	He wants you all for himself and to let all the other men know you are not available.
He wants to be exclusive.	He wants just you and has decided no other women are for him.
He doesn't push you for sex.	He takes you seriously, but seriously wants you.
He wants to marry you!	He doesn't want anyone else.

But He Acts Interested Sometimes

And, maybe the coast is clear just because the psycho killer stopped banging on the door. Don't get sucked back in by mixed signals. He may not want to give up his piece on the side (if you've been breaking the rules I laid out earlier). He

Chapter Seven

might actually enjoy hanging out with you . . . as a friend or for your lady center. None of that makes this a safe space to venture into if you are expecting a commitment.

He is going to give you signs about where he is as it concerns you. A lot of those signs will be in the arena of sex. Either he will keep coming around looking for physical gratification without satisfying any of your emotional needs or he won't pursue anything physical with you and keep you at an emotional distance. One says he's only about the sex; the other says he's not sexually attracted to you.

Sarah's story is a good example of a guy just out for sex.

Sarah

I had a beautiful, newly-divorced woman come to me crying that a man she went on five dates with used her for sex. Sarah told him right before she had sex with him that she wanted a long-term, committed relationship. He told her he wanted a long-term, committed relationship too. So, she gave him her lady center.

The next day she decided to see if he had taken down his online dating profile, and he was still active. She called a friend who was on the same dating website and asked her to try picking him up. Sure enough, he was ready to go out with her friend.

I don't understand why any woman would believe what a man says right before he's about to put his penis in her lady center. He's not going to say, "I just want to put my penis in your lady center, so I'm going to tell you whatever you need to hear to make that happen. When I'm done putting my penis in your lady center, I may call you again so I can put my penis in your lady center another time, but that's all I'll be looking for. Oh, and I'm still dating, so I'm still going to try to put my penis in other women's lady centers too."

NO, NO, NO, NO, NO, Pretty Flower! *Don't go in that room!*

You cannot count on a man to think clearly or act respectfully when his little head has been activated and is doing all the thinking for him. And, if he is on the fence about you, he is going to think there is no reason not to have sex with you right now. It's a win-win scenario for him. If it turns out he likes you, he will keep you around *and* get sex right away. If you don't really do it for him in the relationship department, at least you did in the bedroom.

I'll cut the guy a little slack in that he probably didn't straight out lie to Sarah. Maybe he did want a long-term committed relationship, just not necessarily right then and maybe not be with her.

If you are going to date online, have a buddy system. Get your friends to join too so that if you begin a relationship with someone through a site and it gets serious, you can easily get all the information you need to see if your guy is following through on his commitment to you.

A man who likes you won't be looking for other women. If a man you slept with is still looking for other women, run as fast as you can in the opposite direction! You do not want to stick around to see what kind of fresh hell that will bring into your life .

And, then there's Mindy who is a case study in the guy who just isn't attracted.

Mindy
Mindy was a beautiful woman who came to me about her boyfriend. He wasn't trying to have sex with her and didn't make any sexual advances at all. My first thought was, *He's gay*. She had to convince me that wasn't the case. Mindy's boyfriend was thin, semi-attractive, and in pretty good shape, and she was overweight. When she finally asked him why he wasn't making sexual advances, he told her he was embarrassed about his penis. He had a very minor deformity

that most women wouldn't notice or even care about since it was in working order, but it bothered him.

I didn't understand why he couldn't pleasure her sexually. If he were having a penis issue, there were still lots of fun things a man could do to a lady center that are enjoyable for both parties. Poor Mindy was left sexually frustrated all the time.

A woman needs love and sex as much as a man. Her lady center worked just fine, and needed some pleasure after a year of dating. He never even touched her breasts (she had fabulous D cups). I thought it was pretty selfish of him not to think of her sexual needs, and I was sure he was lying. I'll concede that the deformity probably was a sensitive issue for him, but he wasn't the only one in the relationship.

Then she shared with me that she actually had given him oral pleasure a few times. WTF?! Now, I really had more questions. Her boyfriend told her he didn't want sex because he was embarrassed about a minor penis deformity, but he let her give him head. I walked her through some basic anatomy, pointing out that her eyes were near her mouth, whereas her lady center was not. She could see the deformity while giving him a blowjob, but she wouldn't see it while having sex. I even went so far as to take out a measuring tape to demonstrate for her, in case she couldn't tell from her vantage point just how much closer her eyes were to her mouth. I won't go on about this here the way I did with her because I think you get the point. You do, don't you? It's not obvious to just me, right?

I'm bringing this up because I want everyone to stop making excuses and believing the stupid things men say because you really like him and are hoping there is more there than he is actually giving you. I understand when you are in a situation with a man and many aspects of it are great, it's hard to leave. But, sex is really important in a committed relationship. It's bonding and super fun! It is also a really good barometer for where your relationship stands. If he is engaged *and* respectful, you can be confident in deepening your relationship. If he only shows up for sex or seems oddly uninterested in it or only wants his needs met, you have a lot to worry about.

In Mindy's case, her guy broke up with her a few months later. She was sex-deprived for a year and a half while still giving him pleasure, and ended up without the guy in the long run. It's never worth it, pretty Flower, to compromise your standards and sacrifice what you need to try to keep a guy who may not stick around once he gets what he wants.

To Choo, or Not to Choo

Let me put this in terms you might understand if you love great shoes as much as I do.

Say you are at a Jimmy Choo boutique with your boyfriend and he says you can pick out a pair of shoes, but he wants a long-term committed relationship with you in exchange.

If you don't really like him, you must deny the shoes. I feel your pain, pretty Flower. That's a tough offer to pass up, but you can go and get your own Choos. It's all good.

If you do really like him, get those shoes, girl! And then, please come over and show me! You never deny a gift from a man you love and who loves you too. It's rude!

If you are on the fence about him, you have a more difficult decision. Do you take the shoes or not?

Here's where I'm going with this analogy: You know a man will take the offer of your lady center even if he is on the fence. In fact, he will most likely take you up on it even if he doesn't really like you.

When the feelings aren't clear, it is just as hard for him to pass up your lady center as it would be for you to pass up a fabulous pair of shoes. Don't feel guilty if you struggle with the decision. It's normal. Just remember that there are strings attached and you may not like how they affect the way those shoes fit.

Facing Rejection

For many people, they'd rather be shredded by Freddy than go through the emotional shredding of being rejected. But, I say, who cares? Rejection is rarely all about you. I've seen some fabulous women sit around guessing or making excuses for why men don't want to go out with them anymore. You can guess all day long why he doesn't want to see you again, but you will be most likely be wrong. It's usually not the reason you think. Even if you ask a man straight out why he doesn't want to see you again, he probably won't tell you the truth. Just accept his reason and move on. It's a waste of your precious time. If he isn't interested, there is no amount of negotiation or spin that will convince him he should like you. Don't humiliate and demean yourself by begging someone to love you. Just move on to someone who will do so voluntarily and eagerly.

Your Fool-Proof Test

It can be so hard to know for sure if danger lurks outside without investigating that scary noise, and a lot of times it does end really badly in the movies. But, it is a risk you have to take in dating. So, here's your fool-proof test: Go out with him on a Saturday night and don't sleep with him. Let him take you out for a nice dinner and don't drink! (Yes, I'm going to keep talking about the dangers of drinking and dating throughout the entire book.) Don't go to his house or invite him over. Make sure you end the date—you're tired and have to get up early the next day. See if he calls you again.

If he doesn't, you have your answer. If he does, go out with him one more time without sleeping with him, and see what happens. If he keeps coming back, he likes you, and he has learned that he has to step up to be with a girl as fabulous as you.

You could actually turn a guy who was just interested in something casual into a man ready to commit. Set high standards for yourself, allow him to get to know you as a person, not a sex toy, and he may realize, "Wow, I do like her." Give him a chance to realize he wants you for more than a "good time."

I had a man tell me that some men think it's deceptive for women to have sex on the first date and then "turn the tables" on him and expect a relationship after. He feels she wasn't honest and she wasn't up front about her motives. He feels that if women are willing to have sex with men on first dates, they should understand it's just for physical pleasure. If she's doing it to get a relationship, she has ulterior motives, and it's not cool. She isn't being honest if she claims she just wants sex, if she's all of a sudden hurt because he doesn't call or ask her out again. She isn't honoring their agreement. I have to say, he does have a point!

This is why women need to be clear with men and with themselves. What do they want from the sexual exchange with the stranger? Be honest about what this really is. If you tell a man, "I'm just here to have sex with you; I don't want anything from you," then go ahead and Ho it up, just use appropriate precautions. But if you want a relationship this is not the way to get one, and it's dangerous emotionally and physically.

THE UGLY TRUTH ABOUT DATING

I'm just going to say it: Dating is a form of prostitution. Don't argue with me, I'm right! The definition of prostitution is engaging in sexual acts in exchange for money or some other benefit. So, if you're not getting paid for sex like the 42 million prostitutes in the world, what benefit are you getting from sex?

When you're dating you want something from the other person, you're just not allowed to say it, so most people lie to each other. Most men usually want sex and some companionship, while most women want love, commitment, and sex.

If a man told you directly he wants sex on a first date, you would probably hit him and leave. If you told him that you want to get married on the first date, he would make a hasty exit.

Prostitution is sex for money. The exchange is clear from the outset. Most people think this exchange is wrong, yet many men hire prostitutes. He wants sex and she wants money—everyone gets what they want because the exchange is transparent.

I actually respect prostitutes more than women who sleep with men to get a relationship. At least prostitutes are honest about expecting money for sex. The woman who gives her lady center away in the hopes of getting more than a possible orgasm was not truthful with anyone, most important, herself.

If you just want sex, have a one-night stand. If you want true love, it takes time to cultivate and can't be expected out of a hookup. If you want marriage you must say the word "marriage" and be clear about your intentions and goals for dating. You won't scare a good man away, but you will weed out the ones who have other priorities.

HELPFUL HINT: If you aren't into a man or know a man isn't into you and you are ready to get rid of him, its super fun bringing up marriage. Watch him squirm and stutter. He doesn't know what the heck to do or say. If you really want to sell it, keep a wedding dress photo on your phone to show him.

If bringing up marriage doesn't get him moving fast

enough, float the word *baby* out there! Tell him how much you want babies and how your clock is ticking away. I'm forty-four and can't have any more children, but I bring up adoption! "I saw this cute little kid from South Africa on a UNICEF Box." The bottom line is, don't waste your time if you know it's not working, and keep finding the humor in dating.

Let's Talk About Unicorns . . . I Mean Good Men

I do know some really good, loving, stand-up men. These guys are out there, but they are rare. You know you've found one when your Spidey-senses aren't going off like they do for the guys who don't like you or the wolves who prowl. You actually feel at peace. You'll sit in your lazy boy enjoying your movie and popcorn and won't mind missing part of your movie because your sweet man can't stand to be without you.

A good man will really pay attention to you. He wants to meet your needs, big and small. He will be respectful toward you. He will listen to you when you're upset and never try to bring you down. He will try to keep the romance alive, even after you've been dating for a while. If you've just started dating, he will be doing anything and everything to be romantic and win you over. He will remember the day you met, your birthday, and all of the holidays. He cares about you and those days mean something to him because they mean something to you. He will be showering you with thoughtful little gifts—not just the chocolate or flowers he can pick up at the gas station on the way to your house—to show he cares. A good man will tell you he loves you every day. He won't leave you guessing about where you stand.

Can you pick out the man in love?
I was having lunch two days after Valentine's day with two women. One woman told me her boyfriend sent her to a spa

for Valentine's day. She got a dozen red roses with a romantic card, a mani/pedi, a facial, and a massage. He made dinner reservations at her favorite restaurant and gave her a Versace wallet at dinner. The other woman told us her boyfriend made her dinner at his house. He had red wine because it's his favorite, knowing she only drank white wine. He made spicy chicken because he liked spicy food, knowing she didn't eat spicy food. He skipped dessert because he didn't like it, knowing that she loved it. He got her flowers from the grocery store and had them on the table, but without a card, and had no gift.

    I don't think I need to point out whose boyfriend is the good man totally in love and making the effort to see that she felt special. Also, I don't think I need to point out who is getting married and who is not. And, in case you might be thinking, *Money can't buy me love!*, you should know, the man who was so thoughtless actually had a lot more money than the guy who went all out for his lady.

    A man doesn't have to be wealthy and do extravagant things for the woman he loves if he just puts forth the effort to be a little creative. If he's desperate, he can pick flowers from someone's lawn (though that is technically stealing and I don't condone it), run her a bath, give her a massage, make her a dinner, buy her wine she likes, make a homemade card that expresses how he feels. It's the thoughtfulness that counts. We all just want to feel loved and appreciated by our man and the older we become the less we need extravagant things. We just want to know we mattered enough for him to put some thought and effort into expressing his love; and, in return, we will give love back in abundance to that wonderful, thoughtful man.

Does he like you?
So here's the $64,000 question: Does he like you? Let's have a little fun with coloring to give you a better picture of your

situation. Yup, it may be silly but sometimes seeing things visually puts things in perspective. In the back of the book you will find a coloring sheet that will help you figure out where you stand. You may want to photocopy it instead of tearing it out of the book or make multiple copies so you can color it more than once.

I recommend taping it to your mirror or somewhere else in your home to refer back to if you're second-guessing how your man feels about you. If your heart ends up mostly black, I think you have a pretty good clue about where you stand. Also, you may want to color a new sheet every three months to check in and see if things have changed. The color sheet may start off red while he's in that lust stage, trying to get your lady center, and turn a bit more black as the relationship progresses.

Okay, I know what you're thinking now, and I'm going to stop you right there, pretty Flower! Don't confront him, shoving your coloring page in his face; simply pull back a little and see how he responds. Maybe you don't respond to his calls and texts as quickly or you aren't as available as usual. Give him subtle clues that he's taking you for granted. Nothing fixes a good man's behavior better than the thought of loosing you. If he's still committed to your relationship, this should get your heart back to red. If he's moving on, it will let you know and you can help him accelerate the process.

Now You Know

If you've had a man who really liked you and you didn't like him in the same way—the man who called you, texted you, asked you out a million times, looked at you with puppy dog eyes, etc.—I want you to remember that feeling. That's how it feels when a man likes you. That's how it should always feel.

But, I also want you to remember how it feels for you when that guy who moons over you won't leave you alone.

Chapter Seven

That's how it feels for the guy you're chasing who doesn't feel the same as you do. If you're not sure he likes you, count on the fact that he doesn't. It's really that simple. We all make something so simple really complicated. When my friends tell me their boyfriend cancelled the date or he hasn't texted or called because he's busy, I hang up the phone. I don't have time to listen. A man who likes you will make sure you know he likes you. His actions will show you he is into you. If he's a good man who wants a relationship and thinks you're a Flower, he's not going to do anything to mess it up.

It's really hard for men to find a good woman too. Men complain to me all the time that they can't find a non-Cray-Cray woman, who appreciates them for who they are. Men feel we are looking for the Bigger Better Deal too!

A lot of super sweet men that tell me women use them and take advantage of them. Like Kanye says, I'm not calling you a gold-digger, but . . . if the Louboutin fits . . . Good men deserve better than that. You don't like it when the players or wolves mess with you, so don't mess with the good, sweet guy.

Hanging out with him and leading him on is not cool. Using him for the things he gives you or does for you is not cool. If he is only in your friend zone, tell him straight out where he stands. Don't let him buy you anything, and you'd better be splitting the check 50/50 if you're going out to dinner. Be a high-value woman at all times.

Just remember, the good guy is what you want. Make sure you're not letting a good man get away only to end up with some player who treats you poorly. You will regret it later on, especially if you're getting older and haven't found anyone. Don't ever settle, but make sure you're not letting a good guy get away.

Let me close with Liz's story. It is the best illustration I know for everything we've covered here.

Don't Go in that Room!

Liz

Liz was dating an amazing man. He was just head over heels in love with her. He was so in love with her it overwhelmed her, so she did what too many women do to the really good guy—she broke up with him. She went back to the scary online dating world and went on a few dates. Her dates consisted of a player who wanted to just sleep with her, a guy with severe allergies who sneezed all over her, a guy without a job, a guy who asked her to split the check, and a guy who asked her if she received alimony from her ex-husband. What a cast of characters!

After a period of failing in trying to find something better, she realized how good she had it and how much she truly loved her former boyfriend and asked him for a second chance. He let her sweat it out for almost an hour, but couldn't stay away from the woman he loved. They got back together and got married. (BTW, she's super lucky he took her back; not everyone gets this lucky! Some men will say too bad, so sad and others will already be snatched up by the woman who wasn't pulling a BBD.)

Liz did establish some boundaries for her husband so she wasn't continuously overwhelmed by his love. My favorite boundary she came up with: He wasn't allowed to hug and kiss her as soon as she walked in the door from work. She had a three-minute rule—she got to use the restroom first and put her stuff away. When he's willing to work together for a successful relationship, that's when you know he really does like you. Don't settle for less.

PART III
"THEY'RE BAACKK!!"
—*Poltergeist II*

How to Avoid Getting Dragged Back In

CHAPTER EIGHT
"Checking In Is Easy; Checking Out is Hell"
—*Motel Hell*

Being Prepared for a Break-up

Whether it's an eternal loop of the same nightmare, the corn maze that seems to have no end, or the funhouse mirror room where there seems to be no way out, seeing our girl go through repeated terrors is agony.

I don't want to see you do the same in your relationships. If you are in a bad, unfulfilling, or, worse, abusive relationship, you need to prepare to get out as quickly as possible. I'm troubled by women who continue to stay with men who aren't fulfilling their needs. I know leaving a relationship is difficult, especially if you feel trapped in some way, but staying just prolongs your misery.

If you need help to leave safely, please reach out to some of the community resources and victim's advocates available. If you're hanging on just because you are afraid of being alone, you might need to go back to school so you can make more money or do something else to boost the self-love you may have lost over the course of your relationship that will give you the courage and strength to demand better for yourself.

If you're dating, you should always be prepared for a possible break-up. Relationships come and go like Botox, and most don't even last as long as an injection will. Sometimes you see it coming, sometimes you don't. But, if you aren't prepared for the possibility, it will hit you harder, whether the signs were there or not.

I mean, we prepare ourselves to enter into relationships, but we rarely equip ourselves for ending them. Sure, it can feel like expecting failure before you get started, but not being prepared can set you up for such devastation that you'll never survive to try again. Obviously, entering into to a relationship is so much more fun than getting out of one. It's not fun breaking up with someone or getting broken up with. But, if you aren't fully prepared for a man to break-up with you, you could say or do the wrong thing. Acting classy and strong when someone breaks up with you is the only way to go.

If you are really sad or angry about it, you shouldn't show it when they are breaking up with you. Why? Because it's not going to help anything at all and will only make things worse. Your tears and pleas are not going to change his mind. And, if a man doesn't want to be with you, why would you want to be with him? Don't chase someone who doesn't want you. If you have to convince someone to be with you, what type of relationship would that be? Why would you ever want to be with someone who doesn't see your value? You deserve and should demand someone who is so in love with you his heart aches to be with you.

Men Fear Tears

When a man breaks up with you, he's really scared you're going to cry and ask a ton of questions he doesn't want to deal with. He is anticipating you will beg him to stay, falling apart and making a scene. In his mind, you are going to be distraught over him because he is such a great man that you'll be ruined by the break-up. He imagines you calling all of

Chapter Eight

your friends, crying for months, forgetting to shower, and sitting in bed eating ice cream because he is so darn special. But, pretty Flower, what would happen if you acted as though you don't give a shit that he broke up with you? Seriously, just say, "Okay!"

What does saying "Okay" do? It confuses the hell out of men! Men have fragile egos. They want to know you still want them and that they're the man, even if they don't want you. If you act like it's just Tuesday and it's no big deal, they take notice. You just made their ego shrink to the size of the Grinch's heart. You made their penis lose two inches.

I'm going to give you two great examples of how women handled break-ups in ways that totally disarmed the men who passed them over.

Toni

Toni's boyfriend broke up with her via phone after two months of dating, which is really tacky and a clear sign he was a boy, not a real man. A man would break-up in person. He did acknowledge this wasn't the best way, saying, "I can't see you to break-up. I don't want to see you cry, because I really do care about you." But, that's still being a chickenshit.

Toni said sweetly, lovingly, and respectfully: "Okay, I'm certainly not going to cry over you, Matt. You know I got permanent eyelashes yesterday, so even if I wanted to cry, it would ruin my lashes, and I'm not doing that. I do need to get my Prada shoes back, so is there any chance you can drop them off this week? You know how much I love those shoes. I'll be in and out this week, leave them on the back porch if I'm not here. Remember, I'm going to Vegas with the girls this weekend and I really want to wear them!"

She acted like she loved eyelashes and shoes more than him and was on her way to Vegas to have fun without him.

Of course, he tried to get her back. A man's ego could never handle the fact that not only was she not all broken up about the news he thought would devastate her, but she was ready to go party with friends right after. He couldn't handle that she didn't even care if she saw him when he dropped the shoes off as long as she got them back. Toni was going to Vegas, not sitting around crying for anyone. Her ex knew he'd messed up and she would definitely have the opportunity to move on in Vegas.

Toni would not take him back because breaking up over the phone showed his character. He didn't respect her enough to end what they had in person; he wanted to take the easiest way out for him, without consideration for her feelings. Thank goodness she had a three-month rule before giving her lady center away, or she might have slept with a boy like this.

Ashley
Ashley's boyfriend broke up with her at the park. He went on and on with reasons he just couldn't be with her anymore. She let him talk and didn't say one word. He got really nervous when she didn't say anything.

After two long minutes of dead silence, she finally said, quietly and humbly: "It's funny, I met a really good-looking, nice man yesterday at Starbucks™. We really hit it off and talked for a long time. I felt kind of guilty about it, especially since I told him about my company and he called me at work this morning. I guess I should thank you for breaking up with me. I have a chance to go on a date with him now."

She walked away and left him sitting shocked on the park bench. Of course, he tried to get back together with her. Can you see how that freaked him out? He expected her to cry and ask a lot of questions about why he didn't want to be with her. That's why he was armed with so many excuses. The fact that she just let him keep talking without responding caused him to show his hand and reveal his arrogance.

BTW, her little Starbucks encounter happened two months earlier, but he didn't need to know that. He texted her, called her, and sent her flowers for weeks, and ultimately begged her to take him back. She made him sweat it out to make sure he got the memo: she's a beautiful flower who will be treated like butter!

Toni and Ashley didn't let the rejection of these men affect what they knew about their true value. Don't get me wrong, going through a break-up isn't easy, but, if you can keep your dignity and self-respect in the process, the better off you'll be.

Have some fun with your break-up like these women did. If you're prepared, you can handle it properly, if not, you may do something that is not classy and shows signs of low self-esteem or low self-confidence. This is an important time to muster up the highest self-esteem and self-confidence you possibly can.

Say "okay" to a break-up and leave; it's that simple. If he loves you he will come back. If not, he gave you the opportunity to find the love of your life. I know it hurts, but this is part of dating. As I've said before, you have to be strong as fuck to date.

Always remember, a man who breaks up with you in a cruel or insensitive way is not the love of your life. A man who breaks up with you, but handles himself and your heart well in the process, has character; and, if he realizes he made a mistake and professes his love, begging you to come back, he could be the love of your life.

You're a beautiful Flower; you don't sit around waiting for a man or take him back without getting exactly what YOU want!

My Boyfriend's Back?

Let's say he does realize what he gave up and wants to correct his mistake; he should be expected to go to whatever lengths are necessary to track you down and win you back. But, you should never go back begging for another chance. I don't make the rules; it just is what it is.

The only exception to this rule is if you broke up with your ex and figured out you made a big mistake. In that case, you can call him, but only once to tell him how you feel, and then you can't contact him again. You must do the same thing a woman does when a man breaks up with her. No texting, calling, emailing, skyping, writing letters, cards, sending gifts, flowers, Post-its, Strippergrams, or any other form of contact. He knows how you feel. You must live your fabulous life while he decides if you're getting a second chance. If he wants to make it work again, he will let you know and come after you again. A man won't let the woman he loves get away; he will marry her.

With men, "Absence makes the heart grow fonder." Men want what they can't have, and if they think they have you they don't want you as much. Unfortunately, it's how it works. If you chase after him it's only going to make your self-respect and self-confidence diminish. Don't do it. Don't ever do it.

A man will realize he messed up and will come back to you, or he won't. There is absolutely nothing you can do to help out his process. It's that simple! Remember, if you truly value yourself and know your self-worth you would never consider pursuing a man.

They respond to the feeling of your absence. They respond when they know you've started dating again. They respond when they know they've lost your heart. They respond when they know you love yourself way more than you love them. They respond when you find love again and

Chapter Eight

they've lost their chance.

Have you ever noticed that when you start to move on your ex seems to know instinctively to get in touch with you? I've talked to hundreds of women, and can't tell you how many of them found that when they started to really like someone else, their ex wanted to give the relationship another try.

If you really love your ex, I'm all for getting back with him . . . if he's truly sorry, professing love, offering a solid commitment, and you get exactly what you want.

If you've dated for over a year or two, it should be a marriage proposal with a large diamond. Don't let someone who hurt you get off easy. Get exactly what you want and need, or what's the point of getting back together?

Pay attention, because this is the most important thing I will say in this book: If a man loves you he will find a way to be with you; he will do anything and everything to make that happen. You don't want to be with any man who isn't chasing you and professing his love.

Peggy
Peggy dated a man for five years who was super rich. He was obsessed with his money, liked being single, and wouldn't marry her. She didn't care about his money; she just loved him, but when he wouldn't commit, after years of being very patient, she said, "Bye Felicia." She wanted marriage and children. Three months later he realized that dying alone with a lot of money is stupid and none of his possessions mean anything without someone to love. He called and texted her repeatedly, but she refused to respond. She was done! He'd had several chances and blew it! He called so much she changed her home phone number and email address. He had told her he didn't want to get married, so she felt there was nothing more to discuss. He started to call her at work and

everyone knew not to put the call through to her. Eventually, she changed jobs because of the nuisance, but he found out where she went and called her at her new job. The first time she answered the phone she hung up on him. He called back and she balled him out and he had to yell over her screaming at him, "I'm calling to ask you to marry me!" She yelled back, "Meet me at the court house tomorrow at 10:00!," and hung up on him. He met her at the court house the next day to get the marriage license. He was waiting for her, as happy as could be, with flowers and, more important, his heart. They've been married for many years now, and he treats her like butter!

The bottom line is guys are stupid sometimes and don't realize what they have until they lose it, and sometimes they care about money or their independence so much that they can't see beyond that, even if they love you. Time apart can make them see your value and they will chase you and hunt you down, professing love and begging to marry you! When you're not getting what you want, you leave. Yup, it's so hard! Peggy's heart was so broken and she had to muster up every ounce of her strength to leave him and say enough is enough. But, she loved herself more than him and eventually got what she wanted.

Alone or Afterthought?

When a man loves a woman she's high up on his priority list. He may be calling and texting way more than you even want him to. He's thinking of ways to make you happy all the time, and trying to have sex with you.

If you feel you are way down on the priority list, you need to leave. You should never feel alone or like an afterthought. You should always feel you come first in his life.

Men respond to actions, not words! If he makes you feel this way don't say anything to him, just take action. Don't respond to his texts for twenty-four hours, and then tell him about the fun things you did when he texts again. When he asks to see you, tell him you already made plans for that night, but you can see him a different night. When you do see him don't even consider have sex until you know you're back on top of the priority list.

You have to teach men how to treat you. The first sign of bad behavior has to have a negative response from you, or he won't know your standards. Would you let your new cute puppy shit on your floor without trying to correct his behavior? No! You tell it no and teach it to go outside. He eventually learns and goes outside. If he didn't learn and continued to go on your carpet, I guarantee you would drop it off at the pound. So don't ever let a man shit on you. Sometimes puppies can't help it, but a man can.

Hopefully you know how to handle a break-up now so you aren't compromising your self-respect and setting yourself up for moving on. If he does come back, just remember, pretty Flower, that it should be on your terms and you have every right to get exactly what you want and deserve out of your reignited relationship.

But, don't count on him coming crawling back to you just because you didn't shed a tear. That only works if you were meant to be together and he just needed a little wake-up call. I'll say it again, sometimes a break-up is the best thing that could happen to you because it frees you up to meet the man you are supposed to be with. In the meantime, you have a lot you can do to give yourself the love and care you didn't get from your ex. Read on to find out what those things are.

CHAPTER NINE
"The Next Scream You Hear May Be Your Own"
—*The Birds*

Masturbation and Other Self-Preservation Tactics

Sometimes, the best thing that can happen in a horror flick is for our girl to do her own thing. In most scenarios, the one who wanders off alone gets whacked, but there are times when being clustered together makes for an easier target. If she can break away from the pack and look after just herself for a bit, she stands a better chance at survival.

Whether you are single or going through a break-up/divorce, being without a companion can be tough. If you don't find ways to fill the void in enriching ways, you will end up making dating mistakes that can be disastrous—jumping back in before you're ready, giving up your lady center too soon because you're horny, or settling for the wrong guy because you're lonely, to name a few.

Being alone for a period could be the best thing to happen to your dating life if you do the right things with that time. You need to take care of yourself emotionally, spiritually, physically, and sexually.

Ladies, we are going to get into some specifics here that might feel a little awkward; but, stick with me because this is important info for you to have. You need time to heal from the heartbreaks, the negative messages, and the self-doubt you've been accumulating your whole life. Let me show you how.

Emotional Healing

Break-ups, divorces, and general dating failures all take a toll on our self-esteem. The only thing that deals such a devastating blow to our confidence and how we value ourselves is possibly the loss of a job. It hurts being rejected, no matter who you are or how good you feel about yourself.

Instead of seeking a quick fix to try to get back what you feel you've lost, take time to heal the emotional injury you've suffered. There is a saying that the best way to get over one man is to get under another. Pretty Flower, I want you to be really clear on how wrong that is. If you are emotionally wounded, that's about the worst thing you can do . . . except maybe go get a new haircut.

Give yourself time to recover. Do kind things for yourself. Give yourself a spa day—get a massage, mani/pedi, facial, etc. In fact, make a day of it with your girlfriends and surround yourself with love and support. If you don't have the budget for a spa, have your friends over and do each other's nails over a bottle of wine and a great movie.

You can go on a mini-vacation and just spend time getting to know yourself again. If you can't afford something like that, just find an area of town you've never checked out before and spend the day exploring.

You might need some counseling if it was an especially hard break-up or divorce. Even though I advised you to keep a brave, strong face when he breaks up with you, in private, you don't have to pretend you aren't hurt. Allow yourself to grieve and get help if you need it.

Another important part of emotional healing is self-exploration. With the extra time you have not tending to the needs of an ungrateful and undeserving man you can develop a new hobby, learn a new language, or discover a new skill. All of those things can open doors to meeting new people (possibly the man of your dreams), enrich your life, and help you grow in ways that will make you even more confident about who you are for when you are ready to date.

Spiritual Healing

Your emotions and your spirit are tied together, but they need separate tending. Emotions can also involve a physical response to an experience. Your spiritual health goes deeper and has an even bigger impact on every part of your life.

When you've been through a difficult break-up or lots of small disappointments in your dating life, if you have not been doing anything to grow spiritually, your emotional responses will continue to be immature and reactionary. Being a confident woman who is comfortable in her own skin comes from spiritual strength.

There are several ways to help cleanse your spirit and nurture it. Sometimes the best place to start is actually outside yourself. Evaluating your surroundings and the people in your life will help you clear away obstacles to your spiritual health.

Did you know everything in your home holds energy? If everything is cluttered, old, and does not reflect who you are today it needs to go, and go as soon as possible. This takes a lot of time and work but is so worth it. It's actually very liberating. If you can afford to hire a Feng Shui consultant, do it! If not, you can read plenty online to help you make room for positive energy in your home—your safe and sacred space.

Another area where you might need to do some purging is in your personal relationships. If the people you have around you aren't lifting you up and supporting you, if they aren't adding to your life positively, you might need to break up with a few of them as well. Just as you shouldn't stay in an unhealthy romantic relationship, there are friendships and family relationships that can really drain you and should be changed for your wellbeing.

Journaling is a great way to determine what you really need in your spiritual life to feel healthy. Writing down your thoughts and feelings helps you to sort out all the stuff that might be contributing to you making bad dating decisions. It also helps you figure out what you don't need in your life.

Once you've done these things, you might want to consider some deeper spiritual work by getting involved in a church or taking a spiritual retreat—whatever fits your belief system or offers something that interests and speaks to you.

Being healthy spiritually gives you a radiance and beauty that is irresistible to everyone, but especially to men who might have caught your eye, but hadn't have noticed you before.

Physical Healing

One of the first things we tend to do when our hearts are broken is to binge on comfort food. The next thing we do is determine we'll go on a diet because we are consumed with self-loathing over the binge. Pretty Flower, this is not physical healing. If you decide you want to eat healthier because you want the extra energy and mental clarity it can offer, then, by all means, start chomping on those veggies. Just don't go after some quick-fix fad diet or make any crazy radical changes. You are just setting yourself up for failure. You might benefit from consulting a doctor or nutritionist to develop a solid, realistic plan.

The same goes for exercise. If you decide you're going to do an Iron Man, hike the Appalachian Trail, or climb Mt. Everest and you've never successfully completed a spin class up to this point, you might be going overboard in redirecting your energies. Get a trainer if you join a gym, or just start by walking and increase your time, distance, and resistance as you are able.

An even better option for improving your physical health is making sure you are getting plenty of rest. Emotional upheaval wreaks havoc on your sleep. You might find yourself restless at night or retreat to bed and sleep for days.

If you haven't picked up on this theme yet, I'll point out that moderation is the key. Find balance for everything you are trying to do to get healthy and you'll have a lot more success.

Sexual Healing

I'm going to spend a little extra time on this section because I've found that most women are pretty good about working on the emotional, spiritual, and physical healing they need after a failed relationship. Very few even recognize they need sexual healing, much less get past their embarrassment to do anything about it.

I know this topic makes some people uncomfortable and many associate it with shame and guilt, but it is important to remove the taboos around it so we can celebrate and honor the great benefits it offers. A lot of people assume those who are single already masturbate, but those of you ladies who are going through the end of a relationship probably need it even more since you no longer have a steady sex partner.

Now, don't let that depress you. Use this time to get to know your body and work on you! I have a lot of female friends who can't have an orgasm from intercourse. If they had gotten to know their lady centers to see what type of stimulation they needed for climax, their sex lives might have been a lot more satisfying.

If you try to go celibate with no means of sexual

release, your relationship transition will be even harder to bear. My friends get really cranky when they aren't having sex. I definitely don't enjoy being around them, but, I'm a friend and I bring them sex toys.

Maureen
Maureen was married for ten years to a man and never had an orgasm. Can you imagine having to fake all of your orgasms for ten years? She was having sex so she never really masturbated and got to know her lady center. When she got divorced the first thing I told her was to go out and get some toys. She needed to learn what makes her climax so she didn't have to spend the rest of her life without an orgasm. She got to know her lady center and now can have an orgasm from sex.

When her ex was putting her through the divorce from hell, I encouraged her to tell him that she faked all of her orgasms, but she got her revenge another way. She moved on from that boy and married a man three years later who makes her orgasm all the time. Remember, something good can always come from a break-up or divorce. God sets this stuff up for us to trust that there is something better if we are patient and learn what we need to learn from the experience. Maureen's divorce pain led her to find her pleasure. You go Flower!

Since you shouldn't be out looking for love until you find it in you, and having sex with people is not going to lead to anything positive right now, it would be so much better for you to masturbate—have sex with someone you love . . . *you*.

There are a number of ways to pleasure yourself. Don't be afraid to do some research and investigate resources that will teach you how and remove the fear and embarrassment of discovering your body and what makes it tick . . . and explode!

Chapter Nine

VIBRATORS
Any vibrator can be effective to aid in masturbation. Try a couple and find one that feels right for you. I personally prefer the Rabbit Vibrator. It is one of the most amazing vibrators out there. It pretty much guarantees an orgasm, which you can't be sure of if you go out and sleep with a stranger. Sex with strangers is risky for so many reasons—he could have something icky, he could be a psycho, he could be an asshole. Why risk that when this handy little device will do the job quite well? Based on my informal research, the Rabbit, in particular, is highly recommended by most women I know and bats .1000 in the orgasm department.

LUBRICANT
Darling Flower, if you are going to use a personal lubricant for masturbation, make sure you use something organic. I'm not very concerned if my food is organic, but I'm very particular about what's going near my lady center!

If you use non-organic lubricants, you're putting chemicals like parabens, glycerin, and petrochemicals in your lady center that can set you up for a nasty infection.

My ridiculous motto: Fuck the organic carrots; I'll eat them and risk pesticides, but only organic things are going near my lady center.

There are a number of reasons to give yourself the gift of masturbation.

FOR WOMEN:
1. Prevents urinary tract infections and cervical infections
2. Can cure insomnia
3. Improve cardiovascular health
4. Lower Type-2 diabetes
5. Increase pelvic floor strength
6. Improves our mood

Don't Go in that Room!

7. Relieves stress
8. We learn about our bodies
9. Can't get an STD
10. Can't get Pregnant

And it's not just for women. Masturbation has numerous health benefits for men as well, so don't be upset if a guy you're dating plays with his manhood all the time. It benefits you sexually, darling flower. It's a good thing; look at the list.

FOR MEN:
1. Manages Premature Ejaculation
2. Prevents prostate cancer
3. Makes his penis harder
4. Improves sperm motility
5. Helps him last longer during sex
6. Reduces nasal congestion
7. Manages depression and stress
8. Strengths the immune system
9. Boosts his mood
10. Helps him avoid STDs and pregnancies

Now, a few more fun facts:
- Did you know May is International Masturbation Month? The retailer Good Vibrations declared it in honor of Surgeon General Jocelyn Elders, who was fired by Bill Clinton for trying to bring masturbation in as part of the sex education curriculum in schools.
- Do you know why some vibrators look like animals? Many sex toys are manufactured in Japan where they weren't actually allowed to manufacture them, so they were shaped to look like animals and made in bright colors to trick inspectors! In 1983 the Beaver, Kangaroo and the Turtle debuted!
- Did you know that September 22nd is International

Chapter Nine

Rabbit Day? Now ladies, that needs to be honored! I think it should be a national paid vacation day; the Rabbit took female masturbation to the next level! The vibrator is designed to give simultaneously vaginal and clitoral stimulation. Thank you Vibratex!

Pretty Flower, it's okay to be in a loving, committed relationship with your vibrator until a good, deserving man is ready to step up and fill in.

HELPFUL HINT: Make sure you have a "Death Friend" if you have any sex toys. Your "Death Friend" will throw out your stash if you die so your kids or mom won't find them. Your family members don't need to be cleaning out your drawers, finding whips, handcuffs, vibrators, sliquid, etc. They're upset enough you're dead; they don't need to see your sex toys too.

SIZE ALWAYS MATTERS

I'm sick of too many men being shallow about women's physical attributes when they are far from perfect themselves; we all are imperfect in some way. I know men are visual and they can't help it, but come on! Men who aren't endowed with a penis that is large and solid as a rock when it's hard, shouldn't be so critical of women about their bodies.

Most women like the big hard penis. It's a fact, just like 2+2 = 4. The first question I ask my friends when they have sex for the first time with a new boyfriend is about the size of his penis, and whether he knows how to use it.

I dated an attractive older man with a small penis for awhile. I really liked him a lot until I figured out he was super shallow and had an ego that did not match his penis size. I accepted his short comings because I really liked him and he couldn't help his genetic lottery shortfall. But, I also know he wouldn't have ever dated me if I hadn't had big breasts and a twenty-five-inch waist.

One night, we were at a bar where the bartender was a beautiful woman, but was flat chested and on the thicker side. I didn't even notice all that until he pointed it out. I just thought she was a pretty girl who gave me wine. My boyfriend commented on the fact that some guys wouldn't date her because of her body, even though she was super pretty.

He then proceeded to ask me if I would prefer to date a man who was good-looking or one with a better body. I asked him who was funnier. When I date, I care about humor more than anything else. I do love a tall man with a big penis, and make no apologies for it, but I would go for the guy who makes me laugh before any other trait, even if he had a micropenis. "Looks fade, funny is forever."

He said the good-looking man and the man with the great body were equally funny. I said what any girl would say who was planning to break up with a shallow man who was short and had a small penis. "I would go with the tall guy with the big penis."

Don't throw stones at glass houses! A shallow man is such a turnoff! Yes, maybe I'm guilty of TMP (too much penis) talk in my book, but it's only because during my forty-four years of living I've seen too many women beyond insecure about their looks as a result of men's shallow comments when they aren't the full prize in the Crackerjack box. Even if this man was tall with a huge penis he shouldn't be picking on some beautiful woman who is not a size 2 (the standard in LA and NY, and size 8 in the rest of the world).

There are exceptions to the penis size rule. I know women who love anal sex. They don't care for the really big penis for a very good reason. They prefer small or average. There are others who don't orgasm from penetration, so size doesn't matter as much to them. In the same way, some men don't like skinny girls with big breasts; they prefer a full-figured woman with a nice round tuchus.

Sandy
Sandy dated a man and was really disappointed when she found out his penis was small. She didn't break-up with him because she really liked the man, and she can't have vaginal orgasms. One day she called me up like she'd won the penis lotto. She told me he gave her oral sex and it was amazing! Amazing enough to marry him. She was a very happy Flower!

Darling Flowers, don't ever feel bad about your penis preferences. A man wouldn't be with you if he preferred some other body type. He knew when you started dating whether you were a size 2 or 10, an A or D cup. A man wouldn't date you if he didn't like your size. If you find his size is not what you want or need, I'm here to tell you it's okay.

The moral of the story here is that men with small penises may learn to become really amazing at pleasing a woman sexually in other ways. There is a key for every lock.

CHAPTER TEN
"Who Will Survive and What Will Be Left of Them?"
—*The Texas Chainsaw Massacre*

Getting Closure and Moving On

Well, she made it to the end of the movie and she's still alive. The temptation is to think everything is okay, but don't relax just yet. It never fails that as soon as everyone thinks the are safe, the demon pops up one last time.

Flowers, don't let this happen in your love lives. I'm talking about what happens when you think you've moved on from a bad relationship and are ready to try again. Inevitably, you'll have a moment of weakness when you are feeling lonely, nostalgic, or just drunk and you'll convince yourself it wasn't so bad and maybe you should try with him just one more time.

You are walking into a trap. As we covered in the last chapter, if he does the work and comes after you to prove he really values you, that's a safer scenario, but if you make the mistake of making the first move—of looking back—you will find danger.

The Zena of it All

Love is not for the faint of heart. The courage it takes to put yourself out there is commendable. A lot of men and women don't want any part of this crazy game of love because they don't want to feel that unbearable pain of ending a relationship. They play it safe so they don't get hurt; you, on the other hand, had the balls to jump in with both feet. You're a lot stronger than you think.

The game of love goes on and on and on until you die. I know it sounds very gloom-and-doomish, but there are no guarantees in life other than death. You may get married and end up divorced. You could find the love of your life and lose him to an illness or an accident. Either way you end up having to start over whether you wanted to or not.

What most women don't realize is you don't have to be a tough-as-nails badass and push through your feelings. You are allowed to feel them. You are allowed to cry. I have so many friends who try to hold it together when the shit is hitting the fan and pretend they're okay. Pretty Flower, you need to know crying is not a sign of weakness and being vulnerable actually takes great courage. Allow yourself to cry and get it all out, and then get up, wash your face, re-moisturize, and get ready for the battle you will face in getting back out there.

You may have unfinished business you have to deal with that will take everything you've got, and this is where the warrior princess in you has to step up.

If you don't know who Zena is, Google her! She's a sexy, badass Amazon warrior princess who fought evil and made men cower. Make her your idol or your spirit animal. She was all woman and never lost any of her femininity while fighting for herself and those who needed her help.

It's also important to remember that even though you have more strength than you realized and you should figure out how to tap into that, you also don't have to go through this by yourself.

Chapter Ten

You're Not Alone

The first thing to remember when you are going through a break-up or divorce is that you're not alone. The pain of love ending is universal. Everyone experiences this awful heart-wrenching pain. It's not just your pain; it's the pain of the world. It's the pain that comes with dating. Ask yourself who you know right now who is experiencing what you are feeling.

Think of all the people you know who are divorcing or had a break-up recently. They feel just as terrible as you. Remember when someone cried to you, and you saw the pain in their eyes? Feel their pain for a second; it's the same as yours. Because we are all connected, you will never be alone in heartbreak. Love is all around you, and so is the loss of love.

Look around you and see who loves you right now, your mom, dad, kids, cat, dog, friends, co-workers, grandma, neighbor, etc. People love you! If you believe in God/Universe/Spirit, he/it loves you too. Best of all is the love you will give yourself. But, you certainly can't be with a man who doesn't.

In a break-up, you've only lost the love of one person. Now is a good time to love the hell out of all those people who love you. Show them how loving and caring you are. Give your love away to others as much as you can. See what can you do to make someone who loves you feel really special today. We tend to take for granted those who love us while we are mourning the loss of some dick who doesn't.

And, get rid of all those unsupportive people making you feel worse. I don't know your specific pain and neither does anyone else. I don't know what is going to help you get over the pain and neither does anyone else. A lot of people profess to be experts in this area, but they're not an expert on you; only you are. I can give you some tips and throw some humor at you to help ease the tension, but only you know what works for you. I won't tell you when to get over it because that happens when you're ready. Sometimes it takes time. Just don't wallow in it and bore the hell out of your friends. If you find it harder than you expected to get over your relationship, you might need to go to therapy or talk to divorce/relationship coaches, but don't keep bringing this stuff up over and over again with your friends. It's not healthy for you or them.

Dealing with Your Break-Up

Here are some tried and true ways to deal with the loss of a relationship.

1. *Face it head-on.* You're a strong flower. Write about the good things and the bad things in the relationship. Own your part in the break-up and learn the lessons in it.
2. *Purge.* Remove all connections to him on social media, put his gifts away or throw them out, get rid of pictures, and delete his number.
3. *Meditate.* Listen to guided meditations on attracting love.
4. *Surround yourself with love.* Spend time with people who love you and pour yourself into those relationships for a period of healing.
5. *Take care of yourself.* Get massages, mani/pedis, facials, exercise, and other things that are physically enriching.
6. *Travel.* Take a weekend trip, with or without friends, to experience a new environment.
7. *Seek a higher-power.* Go to church or get spiritual guidance in whatever form speaks to you.
8. *Get out there.* Attend every social event you can and don't confine yourself to home.
9. *Allow the grief.* Give yourself a designated and limited time (maybe thirty days) to mourn your loss.
10. *Get closure.* Have a Break-up Eulogy!

This is a good starter list, but there are other important things you should do to cope with your break-up in a healthy way.

Chapter Ten

COMIC RELIEF

You definitely need to find humor in your break-up and not cry too long. My conversations with people going through a heartbreak usually go something like this:

"What did you hate about your ex? Was he sloppy?"
"Actually, yeah, he was!"
"Well, now you don't have to clean up after Pig Pen!"
"Did he have a small penis?"
"It could have been bigger."
"Okay, now you have a chance to be with a guy the size of Rasputin!"

Don't know who he is? Neither do I, but I read that his penis is in a jar at the Russian erotica museum, measuring in at eleven inches soft! Can we all say field trip to Russia?

Life is too short to spend time being sad, so look for reasons to laugh no matter what you're going through. Your divorce/break-up is going to suck! I mean, really, really suck, and it will hurt, so you have a choice to make. Are you going to spend your time crying and busting blood vessels around your eyes, or are you going to laugh and give your abs a good workout?

It's so cliché to sit and watch a bunch of sad movies and binge on ice cream and donuts. And, don't get me wrong, that's perfectly fine to do . . . for about a minute, and then it's time to flip the script. Watch television shows that make you giggle and movies that make you cry, but from laughter. Go to comedy shows and hang out with the funny people. It really does help. Laughter will always be the best medicine.

Be serious with your therapist—that's what they are there for. Get all the serious stuff out with them. They know what to do and say to keep you off the ledge. Have your friends and family be the support system for you that raises you up and finds the humor. A lot of people suffer because they can't laugh at themselves. We all are a messy, complex bunch of people here on Earth; see it, embrace it, and laugh at it!

Don't Go in that Room!

TRANSFORMERS, ROLL OUT!

I hate to be the bearer of bad news, but you will probably go through another relationship ending after this one—it's part of dating—and if you don't work on yourself and learn from this relationship, the next break-up will probably be worse.

My job as a Transformational Eulogy Specialist is to help people transform through their pain and have a beyond-fabulous Eulogy party. I'll explain more about this later, but one service I provide my clients is a eulogy to get closure, and there is never a good reason not to have a party. I take your life transitions seriously, but I don't let people wallow in their misery. I don't put up with victim mentality, and I'm not the person you should see if you are just looking for someone to let you whine. I'm the person who dishes out the tough love while we drink wine and laugh our way through your pain. I personally like to do all that while sitting in a cemetery to put life in perspective.

There is too much joy to be found in life to sit in a pool of misery. Every chance you get to live should be honored, appreciated, and enjoyed.

HELPFUL HINT: Go find a 95-year-old woman and a 5-year-old to talk to about your break-up, and see what they have to say. I bet their less-complicated perspectives will be a welcome change.

ALWAYS LOOK AT THE BRIGHT SIDE

I'm truly sorry if you're going through a divorce or break-up. Sometimes it feels better being really hurt or sick than going through the emotional pain of a relationship ending.

Always remember, there is a reason that this is happening. Unfortunately, you just can't see the reason now. I wish you could see the reasons you're experiencing this pain, and see the good it will bring you in the future while you're going through it, but that's not how life works.

Chapter Ten

Jen

My friend Jen went to take a walk through her big beautiful home that she was moving into on the Saturday after her big wedding. She found her fiancé having sex with a woman in her bedroom. Obviously, the wedding didn't take place. You can imagine how distraught she was. Six months later she met Joe. Joe was everything she wanted and more. He was a man, not a boy like her fiancé. They are now very happily married with two children.

Everything happens for a reason. When Jen was crying for months, distraught over her ex-fiancé, she might not have cried so much if she had known Joe was coming. All that pain made her stronger, and she appreciates the amazing man she has now so much more.

Tara

Tara had a girlfriend for two years who broke up with her, and she was pretty upset. Her ex had very small breasts, and Tara decided her future wife was not going to be flat chested. It made her feel better to laugh about the small breast issue and have hope that the next woman she fell in love with would have great big, fabulous DD breasts.

You always need to look at the bright side and find even the smallest bit of humor in your pain. FYI, her next girlfriend did not have DDs, but she had pretty fabulous Cs.

NOTE: Nobody wants to shag sad people. Even a really bad guy won't fuck you if you're crying.

FIND WHAT MAKES YOU FEEL LIKE A BEAUTIFUL FLOWER

Does running make you feel good? Does sewing make you feel better? Do you cook? Dance? Think about whatever gives you a break from feeling lousy and spend some time doing that. Go for a jog, make a fabulous new dress, prepare some meals for your elderly neighbors, go to a club. Anything! Do as many things as you can that make you feel good every day.

Just stay away from things that make you more depressed like drinking, smoking, and binge eating. Well, only do them in moderation, at least. Pole dancing and Pinot Grigio takes all my pain away. Although, one tearful night I drank and pole danced and fell upside down off the pole. My knee turned black and I couldn't walk for two weeks. Learn from me, sometimes things make you feel better individually but don't have the same result when combined.

DELETE HIS NUMBER AFTER YOUR BREAK-UP
Do not keep his number. You don't need it (as long as you don't have kids together). It will help in case you are tempted to call. Drinking is usually the way we get over some bad break-ups, and for some reason it seems like a brilliant idea to text or call your ex when you're drinking. Maybe, in your drunken haze, you are convinced you've finally come up with the exact words you need to tell him about how you feel. But, that drunk dialing you are going to do is only going to make you look Cray-Cray. Friends don't let friends drunk dial.

YOU CAN'T BE FRIENDS RIGHT AWAY
I still love my exes and talk to most of them. You spent time with these amazing humans and, in many cases, your break-up doesn't make them not good people, just not the right ones for you. I even give some of my exes relationship/divorce advice. But, let's be clear, you can't expect to be friends right away. Those feelings don't go away immediately, even if you are the one who broke up with them, and it takes time to heal.

I get really happy when I hear my ex has a new girlfriend, or that he's getting married, but that is not something I would have been able to manage right after our relationship ended. That takes time and distance. If you're not truly happy when you hear about their happiness, then that is a good sign friendship is not possible yet. And, let's be honest, if you still have feelings, the friend excuse is bullshit; it's just a way to avoid having to let go of the relationship.

A final caveat to this: Don't stay friends with an ex who lied or cheated. I'm friends with all of my ex-boyfriends except for one. After I broke up with him, I found out he cheated and lied throughout the entire relationship. I have a lot of friends, so I certainly don't need one who endangered my heath and lied to me. It was a long time ago, and I'm over it now, so I can wish him and his small penis joy, love, and happiness . . . just not around me.

Your Ex Isn't Jesus

When the loneliness sets in and you are having moments of weakness, you may begin convincing yourself your ex was not that bad. Everyone does it. When you were in the relationship with them they were driving you insane with all the horrible things they were doing, but now that you are no longer together, you selectively remember the good times: the romantic dinner he made on the roof of your building, the time you flew to Catalina to eat pancakes, the trip to Palm Springs where you tied him up in a chair and had sex, the time you were sick and he brought you candy, soup, and flowers, and the perfect proposal at the Beverly Hilton.

You forget that he worked all the time and left you, didn't clean up after himself, treated you like he could take you or leave you, started to be distant, put you last in his life, lied, stopped saying "I love you," was less attentive in sex, or whatever the case may be.

When people die everyone says really nice things about them during the Eulogy, even if the person was a real asshole in life. No one is Jesus, Buddha, or Krishna, but we tend to remember them through rose-colored glasses when they are gone, and overlook a lot of the pain that they caused us. Take your ex down from the pedestal where you put them and stop drinking the Kool-Aid.

Nobody is a completely terrible human . . . NOBODY! Everyone has a little devil on one shoulder and a little angle on the other. Your ex does have good qualities, but their bad qualities were apparently enough to outweigh them, and that is why you're not with them anymore. You can't stay with the man who listens to the devil more than the angel. Unless, he's well-endowed. KIDDING! I was just trying to see if you're still with me.

BREAK-UP OR BREAK?
Before I throw you a fabulous Eulogy party for your break-up, please make sure it's actually a break-up and not a break. According to most research, fifty percent of couples break up, and then get back together again. Time apart can be a really great thing for relationships and break-ups can actually strengthen your relationship, leading to lasting love.

If you're not sure if you really love your partner, a break-up can help you figure that out. As they say, "Absence makes the heart grow fonder." If you still think of your partner and miss them every day after a few months, it's probably love. You'll definitely value each other more after time apart and gain a new sense of appreciation for how wonderful that person really is.

We're becoming a society that thinks a partner should be able to fulfill 100% of our needs, when realistically it should be around 75%. Online dating is online shopping for the perfect person who doesn't exist. We are not investing in people and relationships anymore. So, a break-up can light the fire of change. You may value your partner more, make sure their relationship needs are met, and communicate your needs more. You may come to realize you don't want to lose this person ever again. Simple small changes can be powerful. Perhaps the first time around you didn't see the need to change to make the other person happy, but you're ready for commitment now. You realized that time alone wasn't that great without the one you love. You realized you don't want to spend the rest of your life alone, and the grass certainly wasn't greener on the other side of the fence. Maybe you didn't even find grass on the other side of the fence, just a bunch of artificial turf.

I'm sure you'll pick the right side of the fence whatever side you chose. If you do choose to get back with your ex, please nurture and care for the relationship so it never ends again! If you choose not to get back with your ex, I know there is an amazing person out there that is worth waiting for.

CLOSURE
Closure is something only you can give yourself. You have to decide when the door is shut. Remember, your ex may not want to hurt you and tell you the truth about why he can't be with you. If he cheated on you he probably feels badly about it, but won't admit it, or feels justified by blaming you for his indiscretion. People don't like to admit affairs or other wrongdoings. Know that it doesn't matter what happened, what matters is that they're not here and you need to be okay with it somehow.

BTW, don't use the need for closure as an excuse to see your ex again. People get closure after the death of loved ones all the time. They're obviously dead and can't give you closure. You don't need answers from your ex when deep down inside you already know the answer.

If you reach out for closure and they don't respond, you will feel worse, and if they do humor you and talk to you, you probably won't get what you need from them anyway.

There is a need for closure after a divorce or break-up, but it comes from inside you. It's imperative to have a Eulogy after the loss of a spouse or partner, whether through death or divorce. A Eulogy helps us attain the closure we need to move on with our newly-altered life. A Eulogy can help us make peace with our new existence and ourselves.

Unfortunately, most people will experience the heart-wrenching pain of a break-up at some point in their life. Psychological research shows that divorce and break-ups warrant the same emotional response as death or the diagnosis of a life-threatening illness. Yet, divorce and break-ups are usually treated callously. Often people are not given the time or emotional space needed for bereavement, to mourn the loss of what once was. Unfortunately, "Divorce Eulogies" or simply Eulogies for any kind of emotional closure are not yet enthusiastically accepted. I'm here to change that!

My company, The Beverly Hills Eulogy, is all about helping people get closure to start a new life. Yes, our services are fabulous, and, yes, they cost a pretty penny. So what can you do if you need our services but can't afford them, or don't live near Beverly Hills?

MAKE YOUR OWN EULOGY!
1. Set a date for your Eulogy about a month after your divorce or break-up. Send out real invitations—this is serious. None of those tacky invitations online. Require all guests to dress in black and bring a casserole for your loss. My Eulogies have strict rules, but yours don't need to. Make it a proper ceremony to help transcend your feelings. Make it fun, with serious undertones—it's even more fun with a lot of alcohol and marijuana (if it's legal in your state).
2. While preparing for your Eulogy, work on getting yourself back together. I always recommend visiting a cemetery to fully appreciate the gift of life. Find your "joie de vivre" as the French say—your love of life. I also recommend you do things that you're afraid of or hate. Go hang-gliding, pet a goat, hold a snake, go parachuting, go scuba diving, ride a horse, eat a new weird food; the options are limitless! It's the perfect

time to shake things up a bit and challenge yourself.
3. Decide how do you want to perform your Eulogy. Will your Eulogy be a traditional speech? Or are you going to sing in a band that you have hired? Will you dress up like the Good Witch of the West or like Scarlet O'Hara in Gone with the Wind? Or will you wear your bathing suit and read Rumi in front of the crashing waves of the Pacific Ocean? The sky is the limit . . . no, your creativity is the limit. You can sing your Eulogy, write a poem, rap it, play the flute, sculpt it, or paint it. It's up to you! It's your Eulogy.

The ultimate take-away from all of this is that no matter what circumstances brought you to this place, if you learn the lessons life has for you in this experience, celebrate the love you've received, cling to the hope of what waits for you, and give yourself time for the healing you need to try again from a stronger place, the wheel will turn back in your favor and you'll live to love again.

It was actually difficult finding stories of really good men while I was writing this book. Everyone had several horror stories and a few had funny stories, but not love stories. I had to put it down a lot because I started to get a bit jaded. Then, as my editor and I were rushing to get my book done before the holiday, she told me we would have to work around her travel schedule because it was her parents' 50th wedding anniversary and people were coming from all over the country to celebrate. I really needed to hear a love story like that—to know that people do stay together and love for a lifetime. They weren't just acknowledging the longevity of a relationship because some do stay together, but miserably so, and that's certainly not anything to celebrate. They were honoring fifty years of love and family and legacy. Love happens, and when you love yourself and wait for it, it will come if you believe it will.

There is an impossibly steep section of the Alps between Austria and Italy, called the Semmering. The tracks were built before there was a train that had the ability to travel up such a steep grade. They had faith in the possibilities. I want you to do that too, pretty Flower!

I Hope You Find Love

I'm a hopeless romantic and I want all women to find the love of their lives. I believe when you truly love yourself and know what you want and deserve, a good man will come into your life.

I want you to have the kind of love that makes your heart race, your hands sweaty, and your head swim—the kind of love where you can't sleep at night because you can't stop smiling as you think about your beloved and where you can't eat because nothing smells as good as they do or tastes as sweet as their kisses. I want you to be so in love that you are obnoxiously skipping and singing through your day!

You deserve that love, but it starts with loving you more than anyone else. I want you to weed out the boys who don't know how to love and aren't nearly good enough for you. I want you to always remember: You're a beautiful flower who deserves to be treated like butter. And never settle for less.

I want all women to learn to respect themselves and not put themselves in a position to get hurt. You should always do what is best for you and your body first. I want you to date with clarity and use your intuition. Pay attention to those little gut feelings you get so you don't get blindsided by a man who isn't honorable.

I hope, if you get your heart broken, you don't suffer too long and find all the humor you possibly can in your situation. I hope the pain turns you into a more loving person, and opens your heart more, instead of closes it.

I truly wish you the only thing that makes life worth living: LOVE.

ACKNOWLEDGMENTS

I'd like to thank you for taking the time to read my book. I hope I gave you a few tips or things to consider when you date. If I didn't help you at all, I know I at least made you laugh a few times. Laughter will always be the best medicine. Now, I'm going to thank my friends like I just received an Oscar because they let me into their private lives for years for my research, and I never got to thank them for all the love and support they've shown me over the years. We all need a beautiful successful talented friend to have as a role model and for motivation. I'm lucky to have a lot of beautiful friends.

Mary, thank you for always being a good friend, making me laugh, and being a positive influence in my life. You gave me inspiration for this book based with your Flowery ways.

Farah, you're the hardest working, most successful woman I know. You encourage me to work harder every day, and always stand by me in everything that I do. Summer, you gave me Buddhist talks of encouragement through the years that really helped me grow. A day without talking to you is weird. My direct, to the point amazing friend, Rana, I so love you, Flower! Carrianne, we were there for each other for many years. Bev, you will always be a Flower! Reshma, you will be treated like butter.

To my sister Lizzie, you are always there to make me laugh; I strive to be as funny as you someday. My amazing friend Dr. Nile, you were the first person I met when I moved to LA, and you took me in at the most difficult time in my life and stood by my side from the day I met you. I couldn't be more thankful. My wonderful friend Marty, our weekly talks and your prayers are what true friendships are about. You're amazing!

Burke, you are a loving beautiful Flower. Cindy, thanks for always checking in on me! Cece, thank you for helping me when I really needed it. It was beyond nice of you.

Jessica, you always make me laugh. Mitra, you're like family to me. Dada and Danny, you are the best people I know; thank you for all your help over the years. Cam, everyone in the world needs someone to believe in them, and you always believed in me. I will be forever grateful to you and need you to know, I believe in you too. My attorney, Laura, you rock flower!

Tony, you are an amazing MAN. I will always put salt on your bread at Woodranch. Deep down you know it tastes better! Jesus, you are beyond fabulous and encouraging. A day without you texting me a penis pic is a day that is not complete. SK, you will always be the smartest woman I know, and have a thinner waist than me. I hate you and love you at the same time. Tavi you are beyond handsome and talented! Evan, you will always be in my heart. Nikos, thank you. Paul, I will always think of you and smile.

Jeff, thank you for all of your help, I love our time together! Eddie, thanks! Elena, you're the best! Christelle, you are a beautiful flower. Stacy, thank you for always being there for me! My psychic, Christina, you're amazing. I laughed when you told me seven years ago I would write a book. (Sorry)! Sirens Media/Leftfield Entertainment, thank you for taking a chance on me . . . Lucilla, you're a flower!

To my beyond-amazing editor, Cara Highsmith, you are such a fabulous flower! Thanks for all of your help.

I'm so blessed to have all of you amazing women and men in my life, to laugh, share, and drink a lot of wine with!

I wouldn't be the person I am without my family at the Agape Spiritual Transformational Center. You accept and love me for exactly who I am, direct choice of words and all. Alice Beckwith told me I would succeed at anything I did; she taught me to always believe in myself, and will always be in my heart.

To my amazing boys, I'm so proud of both of you. Thank you for letting me work a lot and not get too bent out of shape about it. I know I raised you to have values, morals, and to treat all people, especially women, with respect. Your future wives will thank me. I love you more than words can say. You beautiful boys are the reason I know what real love is.

Dad, thank you for always being there for me when I need you and for teaching me what a good, loyal man looks like. You will never see this because you're not allowed to read my book.

ABOUT THE AUTHOR

Annette Marie Westwood is the CEO of The Beverly Hills Eulogy. She is the only Transformational Eulogy Specialist in the world. Known for her luxurious, fun, and unique Eulogy Parties, Annette Marie started The Beverly Hills Eulogy after her divorce to help people transition through loss (mostly divorce) with humor, style, and confidence, and she became an ordained minister to marry her divorced clients when they find love again.

Annete Marie coaches women and men in finding their way through loss of any kind with humor and confidence, and then throws them a fabulous Eulogy party to release the past and move forward. While she loves these aspects of the work she does with her clients, her favorite part is performing second wedding ceremonies. She believes if you learn all the important lessons from your first marriage and work on becoming a better person everyday, you will marry the right person the second time around and spend the rest of your life in a marriage that is full of love, joy, mutual respect, and adoration.

When Annette Marie isn't glued to her computer writing her books or helping a client transition to their new life, she spends her time with her two boys, watching old classic movies, going to the opera and ballet or the emergency room if she tries to cook.

She keeps two things on her desk: a picture of Eminem to remind her not to care what anyone else thinks and always be exactly who she is, and a statue of the Buddha to remember to be thankful for every minute she has on this tiny planet and not get fat and lazy.

Annette Marie lives in Los Angeles, California, with her two sons.

The Beverly Hills Eulogy

The Beverly Hills Eulogy is the only private, intimate, true boutique-style Eulogy Party Service. We create stunning, elegant, stylish, glamorous and fun Eulogy Parties to celebrate you and release the past. While planning your fabulous Eulogy party, our luxury service offers: Life, Divorce, and Dating Coaching, Fitness Training, Makeovers, and so much more.

We provide rituals that have been used throughout history to give closure from the loss of a person through death. You have lost part of your life from your transition, and we believe you have the right to grieve this loss and celebrate your new life. We specialize in Divorce Eulogies but work with those who are going through any life transition.

A Eulogy Party is a way to find your peace in the comfort of friends and family. Our mission is to help you obtain closure from the pain and suffering, or relief and joy that life transitions bring. It is a chance to say goodbye to your Ex-husband/wife, Ex-boyfriend/girlfriend, retirement, health issues, loss of a pet, or just to celebrate how fabulous you are!

We only take on a limited number of exclusive clients in order to make sure our service to you is at the highest standard possible. Please be selective with the friends and family that you invite. This is your upscale party and time to shine.

Please visit our website at www.thebeverlyhillseulogy.com or contact her at annette@thebeverlyhillseulogy.com for more information.

RECOMMENDED READING

You should not be dating until you have read all of these books twice!

He's Just Not That Into You: The No-Excuses Truth to Understanding Guys by Greg Behrendt

Ignore the Guy, Get the Guy - The Art of No Contact: A Woman's Survival Guide to Mastering a Break-up and Taking Back Her Power by Leslie Braswell

Why Men Love Bitches: From Doormat to Dreamgirl - A Woman's Guide to Holding Her Own in a Relationship by Sherry Argov

Act Like a Lady, Think Like a Man, Expanded Edition: What Men Really Think About Love, Relationships, Intimacy, and Commitment by Steve Harvey

Read these two spiritual relationships books as well!

The Vortex: Where the Law of Attraction Assembles All Cooperative Relationships by Esther and Jerry Hicks

The Mastery of Love: A Practical Guide to the Art of Relationship: A Toltec Wisdom Book by Don Miguel Ruiz

This is the book that I give to everyone during transition. It's a must read! Don't be cheap buy the hard copy!

Oh, The Places You'll Go! by Dr. Seuss

WHAT'S NEXT?

If you enjoyed reading *Don't Go in that Room!*, stay tuned for my next book:

Goodbye To You

A Girlfriend's Guide to Wake You Up Before You Go Go Through Divorce

Does he like you? How much?

His name: _____

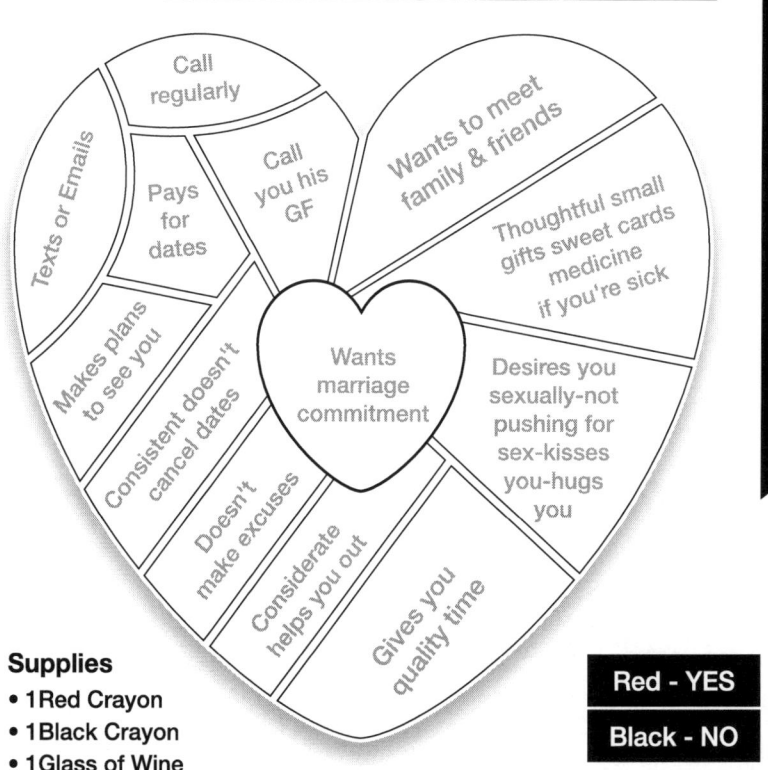

Heart sections:
- Texts or Emails
- Call regularly
- Pays for dates
- Call you his GF
- Wants to meet family & friends
- Thoughtful small gifts sweet cards medicine if you're sick
- Makes plans to see you
- Consistent doesn't cancel dates
- Doesn't make excuses
- Considerate helps you out
- Gives you quality time
- Wants marriage commitment
- Desires you sexually-not pushing for sex-kisses you-hugs you

Red - YES
Black - NO

Supplies
- 1 Red Crayon
- 1 Black Crayon
- 1 Glass of Wine

Instructions:
Please pour one glass of wine. Color RED if it's a YES and color BLACK if it's a NO. This is how he feels about you pretty Flower!

Made in the USA
Columbia, SC
15 February 2022